BRITISH ARMY
AVIATION
IN ACTION

BRITISH ARMY
AVIATION
IN ACTION

From Kosovo to Libya

Tim Ripley

Pen & Sword
MILITARY

First published in Great Britain in 2011 by
Pen & Sword Military
an imprint of
Pen & Sword Books Ltd
47 Church Street
Barnsley
South Yorkshire
S70 2AS

ISBN: 978-1-84884-670-8

A CIP catalogue record for this book is
available from the British Library.

Typeset in 11/13pt Palatino by
Concept, Huddersfield, West Yorkshire

Printed and bound by
Replika Press Pvt. Ltd.

Pen & Sword Books Ltd incorporates the Imprints of Pen & Sword
Aviation, Pen & Sword Family History, Pen & Sword Maritime, Pen &
Sword Military, Pen & Sword Discovery, Wharncliffe Local History,
Wharncliffe True Crime, Wharncliffe Transport, Pen & Sword Select, Pen &
Sword Military Classics, Leo Cooper, The Praetorian Press, Remember
When, Seaforth Publishing and Frontline Publishing.

For a complete list of Pen & Sword titles please contact
PEN & SWORD BOOKS LIMITED
47 Church Street, Barnsley, South Yorkshire, S70 2AS, England
E-mail: enquiries@pen-and-sword.co.uk
Website: www.pen-and-sword.co.uk

Contents

This book is dedicated to
Fergus and Joseph Ripley –
aspiring helicopter pilots for the
twenty-first century

Notes

For ease of recognition the place names used throughout are those in general usage in the international media. Many locations in the Balkans, Middle East and Afghanistan have multiple spellings in local languages so confusion often arises.

The ranks attributed to individuals throughout this book are those that were contemporary to the period under discussion, even though many have subsequently been promoted.

Acknowledgements

With thanks to:

This book has only been possible thanks to the help of scores of members of the Army Air Corps, Royal Artillery and other branches of the British Armed Forces who have recounted their experiences or provided assistance to the author on his numerous visits to operational theatres. Many are named below but many others asked to remain anonymous. They know who they are – many thanks to you all. Any mistakes are mine alone.

Bosnia 1995: Major Nick Caplin AAC, 664 Squadron, Lieutenant Colonel John Greenhalgh, 3 Regiment AAC

Kosovo 1999: Major Richard Leakey 659 Squadron AAC, Major Rupert Hibbert AAC HQ KFOR, the 22nd Battery Royal Artillery team

Exercise Eagle Strike 2000, 16 Brigade: Brigadier Peter Wall

Kosovo 2000/2001: 22nd and 57th Battery Royal Artillery, 654 Squadron AAC Pristina Detachment

Iraq 2003: Colonel George Butler AAC, 3 Regiment AAC, Captain J Crook, KORBR, 16 Air Assault Brigade, Commander Brian Meakin RN, 849 NAS

Exercise Eagle Strike 2005: Lieutenant Colonel Richard Felton AAC, 9 Regt AAC

Afghanistan 2006, UK TF: Brigadier Ed Butler, Lieutenant Colonel David Reynolds PARA

Exercise Lightening Force 2009:
664 Squadron AAC Captain Rob Gittoes AAC, SSGT Barker AAC, WO2 Craig People REME

AMTAT Colonel Yoni Griffiths Major Alex Godfrey AAC, Captain Charlie Hillman

32 Regiment RA: Lieutenant Colonel Sebastian Heath and his team

9 Regiment AAC 2010: Major Al Stocker AAC, Major Jeremy Fountain, RCAF, Captain Tom Roberts AAC, AQMS Will Watchorn, REME

JHC: Major General Gary Coward AAC

HQ Director Army Aviation: Colonel Paul Beaver AAC

MOD DCC: Lieutenant Colonel Neil Sexton AAC, Squadron Leader Al Green, Lieutenant Colonel John Boyd PARA

Wattisham
Captain Windsor Bailey REME, 4 Regiment Workshop

DE&S AH IPT:
Brigadier Nick Knudsen, AH Integrated Programme Team Leader
Air Commodore Doug Whittaker, DE&S Apache Programme Team Leader
Colonel David Cooke, Assistant Director Support in the AH IPT
Lieutenant Colonel Phil Davies, the Depth Support Manager Wattisham

AgustaWestland: Geoff Russell, Marc Holloran

BAE Systems: Mike Sweeney

GEC-Marconi: Ian Bustin, Richard Coltard

Lockheed Martin UK: Mick Holloran, Phil Rood

Thales UK: Nick Miller, Kathryn Shaw

Media: Patrick Allan

The author has made every effort to trace the copyright owners of all the images but if any are incorrectly attributed this will be corrected in subsequent editions.

Chapter 1

Introduction – Army Air in Action

Babaji District, Afghanistan: July 2009

During a hot Afghan night thousands of British, Danish and Afghan troops had driven across miles of desert to their assembly points. Within hours Operation Panther's Claw would start with the aim of surrounding and then clearing hundreds of heavily armed and determined Taliban insurgents from the villages and woods around the run-down town of Babaji. Overhead British Army attack helicopters and unmanned aerial vehicles (UAVs) were flying top cover for the approaching columns of armoured vehicles and scouting ahead gathering intelligence on enemy positions and movements. As the month-long battle unfolded, Army Air Corps (AAC) attack helicopters and Royal Artillery UAVs would play decisive roles in the operation, locating and then striking at insurgent bases and fighting positions

Operation Panther's Claw was the largest British military operation since the 2003 invasion of Iraq involving some 5,000 troops, backed by hundreds of Danish and Afghan allies. The mission of 19 Light Brigade was to push into the Taliban sanctuary around Babaji, between the large towns of Nad-e-Ali and Gereshk, and capture all the district's main villages. Other troops were to make surprise moves across the desert to set up cordon positions around the district to trap any insurgents that might try to escape the clearance operation led by the 800 troops of the Light Dragoon's Battlegroup.

As the initial moves were under way, at the main British base at Camp Bastion maintenance technicians and armourers of 662 Squadron AAC were working to prepare its eight AgustaWestland Apache AH.1 attack helicopters for around-the-clock missions. Boxes of 30mm cannon ammunition, CRV-7 2.75-inch rockets and AGM-114 Hellfire missiles were being stacked next to the landing pads and the squadron's pilots had been rested to allow them to dramatically increase their flying or ops tempo during the assault. Two flights, each comprising a pair of helicopters, were scheduled to be in the air as the first troops of the Light Dragoons crossed their start line – the point at

11

which Taliban resistance was expected to be heaviest. Two more Apaches were held back at very high readiness (VHR) at Camp Bastion's heli-pad ready to lift at a few minutes' notice to react to emergencies. This was most likely to be the close escort of a Royal Air Force Boeing Chinook HC.2 heavy-lift helicopter containing medics of the immediate reaction team (IRT) to pluck casualties from landing zones close to insurgent positions.

On the other side of Camp Bastion in an apparently nondescript group of air-conditioned pre-fabricated buildings, Royal Artillery imagery analysts were peering at large computer screens showing live video imagery of the battlefields, beamed from Hermes 450 UAVs orbiting high over Babaji. The analysts were not just looking for signs of enemy movement or insurgents planting deadly improvised explosive devices (IEDs) along the Light Dragoons' intended line of advance but they were also watching for signs of unusual behaviour among the local population. This so-called pattern of life analysis would tell them if the British had lost the element of surprise and the degree to which the population were helping the Taliban.

AAC Apache AH.1 attack helicopters have proved their worth time and time again in combat in Afghanistan. (AgustaWestland)

Afghanistan's demanding climate and environment test AAC helicopters and pilots to the limit. (AgustaWestland)

For the Gunners of 22 Battery Royal Artillery, this was no remote control 'video game'. Several of their comrades were with the advance guard of the Light Dragoons, sweating under the weight of heavy body armour, water containers and hundreds of rounds of SA-80 rifle ammunition. Crucially, they had video receivers that allowed the senior officers of the Light Dragoons to watch the same video feed as the analysis team at Camp Bastion. Other Gunners with the Light Dragoons assault troops were standing by ready to launch Lockheed Martin Desert Hawk III mini-UAVs to provide close surveillance over the battlefield. To the troops of the Light Dragoons, the Royal Artillery UAVs were known as 'Greeneyes' and for the next month they would be overhead around the clock giving them an unprecedented view of the battlefield. Unlike some bigger UAVs operated by the Royal Air Force or allied air forces that were controlled from the coalition air headquarters in the Gulf state of Qatar, Greeneyes UAVs were owned and operated by 19 Light Brigade and they could be tasked immediately to meet the needs of British troops, 24/7. Operation Panther's Claw would see all the British Army air assets in Afghanistan used to maximum effect.

13

The operation kicked off on 3 July 2009 and within minutes of the British troops advancing they had called in Apaches to neutralize enemy positions. Over the first week the intensity of AAC attack helicopter operations can be gauged by the fact that 662 Squadron flew 191 hours and fired 3,000 rounds of 30mm cannon ammunition, 10 Hellfires and 24 rockets.

On the ground, the Light Dragoons had to fight for every building and village as they pushed forwards. Babaji district had been heavily seeded with IEDs to such a degree that British Army combat engineers described it as the 'biggest minefield in the world'. The officer commanding 662 Squadron, Major Cook, and his flight of two Apache were engaging two compounds containing six Taliban fighters resisting the Light Dragoons' advance on 6 July when a British Scimitar light tank was hit by a rocket-propelled grenade. As British troops tried to free the vehicle's wounded crew, they set off two IEDs and three more soldiers were wounded, including the forward air controller (FAC) or Joint Terminal Attack Controller (JTAC) with the assault wave. The IRT Chinook was scrambled from Camp Bastion and Major Cook's two Apache were diverted to provide top cover for the extraction mission.

The heavy casualties meant the Chinook had to make three landings to lift off all the wounded men but the landing zone was swept by Taliban fire. So each time the Chinook approached, Major Cook and his wingman flew ahead and put down 30mm cannon suppressive fire into the Taliban trenches. Over a 20-minute period they fired some 600 rounds to allow the Chinook to safely pull out all the casualties.

Royal Artillery Hermes 450 unmanned aerial vehicles are airborne around the clock over Helmand province to protect British troops from insurgent attack. (Thales)

The break-in phase of Operation Panther's Claw comprised just over a week of heavy fighting. Gradually, the enemy began to realize the precarious nature of their position, with British troops squeezing them from four sides, and their fighters started to make their escape. The British, Danish and Afghan battlegroups had set up blocking positions along the series of drainage canals that bounded Babaji district. These canals provide ideal patrol lines for the Hermes 450s and their operators started to spot an increasing number of suspicious individuals attempting to cross them during the hours of darkness. Grounds troops were then dispatched to intercept them or if they were openly carrying weapons then Apache and fast jets were cleared by the UAV operators to engage the targets.

Likely locations for the positioning of IEDs were also kept under surveillance by the Greeneyes UAVs in the build up and duration of the operation, leading to several Apache strikes on Taliban IED teams. During one incident two Apache were directed to where a Hermes 450 had detected several men acting suspiciously. The helicopter crews located the men and watched

Video imagery of Taliban insurgents recorded by Hermes 450s gives British commanders early warning of insurgent attacks. (Thales)

15

Royal Artillery soldiers control Hermes 450 missions from control cabins at Camp Bastion. (Tim Ripley)

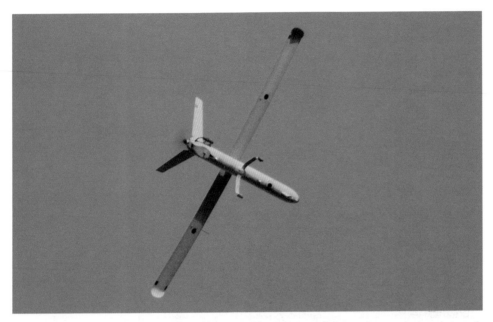

A Hermes 450 flying several thousand feet above Helmand province. At such heights the Taliban have great difficult seeing and hearing the unmanned aerial vehicles. (Thales)

them for several minutes through the Apache's night vision sensors at three kilometres' range until the Taliban gave themselves away as bomb makers. Within minutes, they had been successfully engaged and killed, which caused a major boost to morale among the assault troops who had already taken dozens of casualties from the hated IEDs.

The finale of Operation Panther's Claw got under way on 25 July as reserve troops from the 3rd Battalion, The Royal Regiment of Scotland (3 SCOTS) Battlegroup were helicoptered forward to occupy and secure several villages in the district that had yet to be cleared by the Light Dragoons. This was the battalion's fourth major air assault mission of Operation Panther's Claw. Royal Artillery UAVs generated intelligence briefing packs full of detailed pictures of target areas to allow the assault troops to make detailed plans for their mission. At first light, on 25 July two Apache led six Chinooks into action to land nearly 200 troops. The operation caught the Taliban by surprise and within a few hours the Adera Cemetery area had been secured.

Operation Panther's Claw was a major success of the British Army's integration of air assets – fixed wing, helicopters and UAVs – flying above a complex battlefield. The operation was repeated on an even larger scale in January and February 2010 during Operation Together or Moshtarak in central Helmand province.

For the aviators of the AAC and the UAV operators of the Royal Artillery these operations, as well as the daily missions flown in Afghanistan in between those set piece deliberate operations, graphically demonstrated that the British Army has fully embraced twenty-first century air-land operations.

Forty years earlier, the AAC had begun to ramp up its operations in Northern Ireland. Flying the aging Bell Sioux and Westland Scout helicopters they picked up the nickname 'Teeny Weeny Airways'. The little Sioux and Scouts could only carry a couple of passengers and when compared with the bigger transport helicopters of the Royal Air Force and Royal Navy, they seemed to have only a minor role on the battlefield.

At the end of the first decade of the twenty-first century, the AAC boasted a fleet of some 150 modern helicopters and aircraft – bigger than several European air forces – and the Royal Artillery has more than 100 UAVs in service, with more bigger and better systems soon to enter service, making it the largest and most experienced operator of unmanned systems in the British armed forces.

Two AAC Apache AH.1s are held at very high readiness alert 24/7 at Camp Bastion, ready to respond to calls for help from British troops under Taliban attack. (AgustaWestland)

This book profiles the British Army's airpower, both AAC and Royal Artillery, looking at the equipment they use, how they are organized and how they fight. It examines the major operations of the last decade, which have shaped and moulded the aviators or AAC and UAV crews of the Royal Artillery into some of the British Army's most highly skilled battle-winning troops.

The British Army's front-line combat troops now rarely go into battle without heavily armed Apache flying top cover and UAVs overhead to spy on the enemy. They are also in great demand from allied forces, who value the capabilities, experience and expertise of the British Army's air warriors. Not surprisingly, Britain's enemies rarely stay around when they hear the distinctive sound of an approaching Apache helicopter's rotors or a UAV's engine overhead.

Chapter 2

British Army Helicopters, Aircraft and UAVs

In the first decade of the twenty-first century, the British Army boasted a fleet of some 150 combat helicopters and scores of unmanned aerial vehicles (UAVs). At the turn of the century, the British Army was in the process of a major re-equipment programme to bring new helicopters in to service and develop new UAVs. By 2011 many of these projects were coming to fruition and the Army Air Corps and Royal Artillery boasted equipment that was second to none and had proved itself in combat operations in Iraq and Afghanistan.

Helicopters

Apache

Since May 2005 when the first British Army attack helicopter (AH) regiment was declared combat ready, the AgustaWestland Apache AH.1 has been the AAC's primary weapons systems. The variant in service with the British Army is derived from the Boeing AH-64D Longbow Apache, which first entered US Army service at the turn of the century. This differs from the original A model Apache, in having the Longbow millimetre wave radar-based weapon system to allow it to engage targets in bad weather or at night.

AAC Apache AH.1s have UK-specific engines, rockets, communications and defensive systems.

AgustaWestland Apache AH.1

Crew:	2
Engine:	2 × 850shp Rolls Royce RTM-322
Length:	9.53m
Height:	10.3ft
Maximum speed:	330kph

Cruise speed:	272kph
Range:	462km
Armament:	16 × AGM-144 Hellfire missiles (including AGM-114N1 Metal Augmented Charge (MAC) variant) 76 × 2.75″ CRV-7 rockets, 1200 × 30mm cannon rounds
Surveillance/ target acquisition:	TV (127 × mag), Thermal Imaging (64 × mag), Direct view optics (18 × mag)

The two-seat Apache has seen extensive combat service with the US Army, Israeli Defense Forces, Royal Netherlands Air Force and United Arab Emirates Air and Air Defence Forces since 1989. It has established a reputation as a highly effective and reliable weapon system, thanks to its night vision sensors and precision firepower.

At the heart of the Apache is its two crew – the pilot and gunner – who ensure its sensors and weapons can be used to optimum effect. British Apache are now fitted with the Lockheed Martin Modernized Target Acquisition Designation Sight/Pilot Night Vision Sensor (MTADS/PNVS), which allows the crew to see targets in great clarity at several kilometres'

The AAC's sixty-seven Apache AH.1 attack helicopters are the core of its force and will remain in service for at least another twenty years. (Tim Ripley)

3/2282 50

range. The crew can view the images from the MTADS either on a cockpit screen or have them projected into the eye piece of their helmets. In this mode, the crew can 'slave' the MTADS sensor turret to their helmet so when they turn their head the sensor follows it to ensure the crew can continuously keep 'eyes on target'.

The Longbow radar is the Apache's second sensor system, which is designed to locate and identify large metal objects, such as tanks, trucks and artillery pieces, at several kilometres' range at night or in bad weather. Radar returns can be used to cue the millimetric wave radar guided variant of the Hellfire so the helicopter's crew can target enemy vehicles and heavy weapons very quickly, using a few computer curser movements to identify targets and then launch missiles.

For close-in targets, AAC Apache AH.1s have their 30mm cannons and CRV-7 rockets. The cannon can also be 'slaved' to the crew's helmets and gives them a very rapid response capability if they see suddenly emerging targets and need to put down fire immediately, while rockets are highly

Apache AH.1s boast an awesome array of airborne firepower, including Hellfire missiles, CRV-7 rockets and a 30mm cannon. (Tim Ripley)

The veteran Lynx AH.7 soldiers on in the utility role despite losing its TOW missile capability in 2005. (Tim Ripley)

effective at putting down a spread of fire against large formations of enemy infantry deployed in the open.

The Apache AH.1 is also one of the best-protected helicopters in the world. Both the pilot and gunner sit in titanium seats to give them protection from small arms fire and shell fragments. Other key parts of the helicopter are protected by armour to ensure it can keep flying and fighting even after it has been hit by enemy fire.

A defensive aid suite (DAS) is fitted to detect heat-seeking and radar-guided enemy surface-to-air missiles (SAMs). This then can automatically launch flares to decoy heat-seeking missiles and chaff to put radar-guided weapons off their track.

The basic tactical grouping of AAC Apache is the pair of helicopters, flying together on the same mission. On patrols, this grouping allows one Apache to provide cover or overwatch as the other helicopter moves closer to targets to observe them better or get a better shot. Two pairs usually operate together and are known as a flight.

Up-engined Lynx AH.9As have given the AAC's utility force a new lease of life to bridge the gap until the Lynx Wildcat enters service in 2014. (Tim Ripley)

In turn, an AAC squadron comprises two flights' worth of aircrew and around 100 maintenance and support personnel, including some 50 technicians from the Royal Mechanical and Electrical Engineers (REME). They have the vital task of keeping the Apache's complex systems working at peak efficiency.

Lynx

The veteran Westland Lynx AH.7 was once the AAC's main armed helicopter. It has now been replaced in the anti-tank role by the Apache and now is used primarily for manned airborne reconnaissance, small-scale troop transport, command and control and casualty evacuation.

The Lynx AH.1 entered service in 1978 and the armed AH.7 started to be deployed in AAC regiments in Germany in the early 1980s. Both the AH.1 and 7 variant had skids. The wheeled AH.9 variant is the newest example of the Lynx in AAC service. This variant was never armed with the TOW missiles.

The Gazelle AH.1 has provided sterling service as an observation helicopter for over forty years. (Tim Ripley)

Nitesun searchlights were developed for use in Northern Ireland from Gazelle and other AAC helicopters. (Tim Ripley)

The AH.7 variant is to be replaced from 2014 by the Future Lynx or Lynx Wildcat and the upgraded AH.9A variant with more powerful engines is to remain in service until the end of the decade.

Westland Lynx AH.7/9

Crew:	2 (3 with door gunner) + 8 troops
Engines:	2 × 850shp Rolls-Royce Gem 41 (LHTEC CTS800-4N on AH.9A)
Length:	12.06m
Height:	3.4m
Maximum speed:	330kph
Cruise speed:	232kph
Range:	885Km
Combat radius:	Approx 100km with 2-hour loiter
Armament:	2 7.62mm GPMG machine guns or 1 × 0.50 cal. machine gun

The Lynx AH.7 used to be armed with the TOW wire-guided anti-tank missile until early 2005 but this was withdrawn from use after the arrival of the Apache. These helicopters have now been stripped of their missiles launchers and targeting systems.

Defender and Islander aircraft are the only fixed wing aircraft in AAC service, flying in the manned aerial surveillance role. (Tim Ripley)

The Phoenix saw service with the Royal Artillery for a decade from 1998 and brought the British Army into the modern era of unmanned systems. (BAE Systems)

Since 2007, the Lynx AH.9/9A has been equipped with the L3 Communications MX-15 turret and data link to allow live video imagery to be downloaded to ground troops equipped with laptop-sized video receiver terminals.

On the battlefield, AAC Lynx also operate in pairs to ensure that tactical flexibility is maintained. The Lynx is considerably simpler than the Apache so AAC light utility squadrons usually only require between fifty and sixty support personnel.

Gazelle

Like the Lynx, the Gazelle was the result of Anglo-French helicopter collaboration in the late 1960s and early 1970s. In its time the Gazelle was a very advanced design.

The age of the light observation and liaison helicopter and its limited performance in 'hot and high' environments means it is increasingly relegated to non-combat roles. When the final attack helicopter regiment completed its conversion to the AgustaWestland AH.1 Apache in 2009, the Gazelle were concentrated in 5 Regiment AAC in Northern Ireland on UK-manned aerial surveillance duties.

Westland Gazelle AH.1

Crew:	2 + 3 passengers
Engine:	592shp Turbomeca/Rolls-Royce Astazou 111N2
Length:	9.53m
Height:	3.18m
Maximum speed:	265kph
Cruise speed:	233kph
Range:	670km
Combat radius:	Approx 100km with 2-hour loiter
Armament:	2 × 7.62mm machine guns (not standard)

The Gazelle's observation role means it is equipped with a variety of still and video cameras, as well as search lights to illuminate ground targets. These systems were developed in the 1980s and 1990s for use in Northern Ireland and they have been largely superseded by the MX-15 systems on overseas missions.

Bell 212

The Bell 212 HP AH.1 is derived from the Vietnam-era Bell 205, the Huey UH-1. The Bell 212 HP has a twin engine Huey, but retains the original teetering rotor system of the iconic helicopter. The AAC operates eight Bell 212 helicopters, which are optimized to fly in hot and often humid conditions while also being able to carry considerable loads. A winch on the side of the aircraft also enables medical evacuation in otherwise difficult terrain. The helicopters are currently used by the AAC training detachments in Brunei.

Bell 212 HP AH.1

In service date:	1994
Maximum all up mass:	11,200lb
Engines:	2 × Pratt & Whitney PT6T-3B of 1,800shp
Crew:	2 + 13 passengers
Length:	57ft
Main rotor diameter:	48ft
Height:	14ft
Maximum speed:	130 knots
Range:	250NM
Specialist equipment:	Winch, underslung bucket (for extinguishing fires)

Aircraft

Islander/Defender

The Defender is the latest version of the Britten-Norman Islander twin turbo-prop aircraft and is used in a variety of roles. The Islander was introduced into service in 1989 as a replacement for the ageing Beaver. It is the AAC's only fixed wing aircraft and usually employed in a surveillance capacity, however it also has a limited use in transporting personnel. This aircraft has been extensively used in Northern Ireland, Iraq and Afghanistan. Other roles include air photography, airborne command post and liaison flying.

Islander AL.1

Gross weight:	7,000lb (maximum all up mass)
Engines:	2 × Allison 250 turboprop
Crew:	1 pilot, 1 crewman + 6 passengers
Dimensions:	length 10.93m, wingspan 14.93m, height 4.2m
Maximum speed:	196 knots
Cruising speed:	155 knots
Range:	380NM

In the photographic role the aircraft is handled by a single pilot, while the crewman operates the camera system. The aircraft is a very stable platform; it can carry a useful payload of bulky camera equipment, has a good endurance and is fairly quiet. More recently the aircraft have been fitted with MX-15 camera systems and associated data links.

Unmanned Aerial Vehicles

The British Army has operated three main types of unmanned aerial vehicles (UAVs) since 1998, the GEC-Marconi Phoenix, Lockheed Martin Desert Hawk and the Thales-supplied Hermes 450. These all rely on very different technology and represent a clear progression in capabilities available to the Royal Artillery, which has the responsibility of operating all British Army UAVs.

Phoenix

For nine years, from 1998 to 2007, the Phoenix was the Royal Artillery's primary tactical UAV but it has its origins in the Cold War and many of its limitations can be traced to design requirements specified to meet the needs of fighting the Soviet Army on the North German Plain.

The Phoenix was designed to provide real-time surveillance for the Royal Artillery Multiple Launch Rocket Systems (MLRS), which had the mission of hitting second echelon Soviet tank divisions advancing towards the British Army of the Rhine (BAOR). Work on the project began in 1985 and GEC-Marconi (later Marconi Electronic Systems and then BAE Systems) was contracted in 1987 to build the Phoenix. The system was assembled at the company's factory at Rochester in Kent. Technical problems, delays and cost overruns during its development resulted in the Phoenix being heavily criticized by parliamentarians and the media, making it the cause célèbre of British defence procurement during the 1990s.

The British Army wanted the Phoenix to be able to fly around 50 kilometres behind enemy lines and broadcast back live video imagery of enemy tanks to Royal Artillery commanders, who would then target MLRS strikes to saturate Soviet tank columns with hundreds of armour-piercing bomblets. At the heart of the Phoenix systems was the requirement that the air vehicle, as the flying element of UAV systems are known, could be launched and recovered without the need of a runway. The Phoenix was powered by a Westlake Aero Engines WAE 342 two-stroke, flat twin fuel injection engine,

Live video imagery from Phoenix unmanned aerial vehicles provided a battle-winning edge for the British Army in Kosovo and Iraq. (BAE Systems)

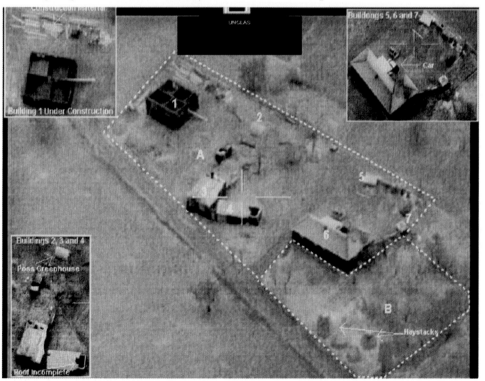

25 horsepower two-bladed propeller that gave it a maximum speed of 104mph and carried enough fuel for five hours' flight, at up to 9,000 feet in altitude. It normally cruised at between 60 and 70mph when on station over a target. Crucially, the Phoenix requirement did not include the need to allow the video imagery to be transmitted from the ground control station (GCS) to other locations such as higher command headquarters. This, along with the launch and recover system, would prove major limitations on the very different battlefields of the twenty-first century. The low power of the engine meant it was ill-suited to operating in hot climates and at high altitudes, where lots of power was needed by air vehicles to fly over high mountains or in thin air.

The Phoenix air vehicle, of modular construction, was manufactured from composite materials including Kevlar and Carbon Fibre/Glass Fibre-Reinforced Plastic (CF/GFRP) sections and Nomex honeycomb panels.

The air vehicle could either autonomously fly a pre-programmed mission or could be piloted by the air vehicle controller in the GCS. Updates from the GCS initiated height and speed changes and for circling, race-track and cloverleaf observation flight paths.

The mission pod was mounted in a sensor turret, on the underside of the landing parachute pod. The two-axis stabilized turret housed a thermal imaging camera providing $60° \times 40°$ field of view. When the Phoenix was orbiting a target, the line of sight could be locked to a point on the ground so the sensor was steered to remain on target. The thermal-imaging night vision camera was designed to allow the operators to identify tanks and other large weapon systems so they had limited utility when used to track individual soldiers or civilians.

The ground control unit consisted of a ground control station vehicle and a ground data terminal towed by a Land Rover. It could be positioned up to 25km from the launch and recovery units.

The ground control station was operated by a crew of three, including a mission controller, air vehicle controller and image analyst. The GCS shelter contained three workstations equipped with high resolution colour displays to analyse and manipulate video imagery. The operator was able to select a thermal image view of the battlefield or a map displaying the positions of the target and the UAV. Up to two air vehicles could be controlled from the same ground control station.

Video was transmitted by a steered, $360°$ J-band radio data link to the ground data terminal and then by cable to the GCS up to one kilometre away. Target data was then transmitted to the forward artillery units by the Battlefield Artillery Targeting System (BATES) directly to the guns, over the British Army's radio network. The position of the GCS and ground data terminal were crucial to the ability of the Phoenix to monitor specific targets and this needed careful planning, particularly in mountainous terrain where direct line of sight to the air vehicle could not be maintained from the ground data terminal. If this was broken then the imagery could not be transmitted and flight control was lost, resulting in the air vehicle automatically returning to base or crashing.

The launch vehicle was the Phoenix 14-ton Foden army truck, equipped with a pallet-mounted lifting crane, hydraulically and pneumatically operated launch catapult and ramp, and a computer to download mission data into the UAV prior to launch. Within an hour of reaching a launch site, the UAV could be assembled and launched. A second UAV could be launched within a further eight minutes.

For landing, a drogue parachute, installed in the tail of the fuselage, was connected to the spring-loaded tail cone ejection plate. The tail cone was ejected to extract the drogue parachute and the engine stopped with the propeller in the horizontal position. During descent, the air vehicle inverted so it landed on its upper surface to protect the mission pod. The force of the landing was supposed to be absorbed by an airbag and frangible fin tips. This landing mechanism was required to meet the need to land without a runway but it proved to be a crucial weakness of the Phoenix. It took a long time to get right and delayed the entry of the Phoenix into service until 1998.

The catapult launch system of the Phoenix gave it great flexibility but the vehicles were big, heavy and could not be moved by air. (BAE Systems)

Desert Hawk mini-unmanned aerial systems entered Royal Artillery service in 2004 and have provided front-line infantry commanders with their own 'eye in the sky'. (Tim Ripley)

In the Balkans and Iraq, landing the Phoenix on rocky ground, in high winds, caused far higher levels of damage than had been anticipated during experiments and training in the UK. This resulted in a far higher consumption of the 198 air vehicles than expected and although many parts could be recycled it meant that once committed to operations from 1999 onwards the need to preserve the scarce number of Phoenix started to limit the willingness of commanders to use them except for very important missions.

An 8 × 6 Foden Demountable Rack Offload and Pickup System (DROPS) container carrying truck was used to transport both the spares containers and air vehicle transport containers to each flight location and also carried the GCS box body. A Land Rover or RB44 light truck was fitted out to carry the Phoenix in its broken down state and was used by recovery teams who collected air vehicles after they had completed missions. The whole air vehicle could be fitted directly into the rear of the vehicle for transport back to the main launch locations to be re-built back at the launch vehicle. The recovery crew then re-tested and made it ready for its next mission.

Desert Hawk

This is a totally differed category of UAV from the big Phoenix. It is classed as a mini UAV because it is hand launched by a single soldier.

The first Desert Hawk Is were ordered from the US defence giant Lockheed Martin in 2003 with urgent operational requirement (UOR) funding to help British troops in Iraq defend their bases from insurgent attack.

At first glance the Desert Hawk appears to be little more than a high specification remote control model aircraft. The Desert Hawk I variant and its successor, the I+, were launched using a bungee spring and could stay airborne for up to an hour. They could fly up to 300 feet in altitude and transmit live video imagery back to a control station up to ten kilometres away. The pilot flies the aircraft by means of an Xbox or PlayStation type control station and an imagery analyst has a laptop to monitor and manipulate video imagery from the air vehicle.

The Royal Artillery's first use of the Desert Hawk I in Iraq was dogged by interference with the UAV's radio data link from the Iraqi civilian mobile phone network and urgent modifications had to be made to allow it to be used in southern Iraq. This problem also inhibited the use of Desert Hawk for training exercises in the UK until further modifications were made in 2008.

In 2005 the UK Ministry of Defence decided to buy a trial batch of the upgraded Desert Hawk III and after a successful trial in Afghanistan an order for $2.65 million worth of systems was made in February 2006. Orders worth $10.1 million were made in 2007 bringing the Royal Artillery inventory to 18 systems with 144 air vehicles in mid 2008. Two years later a follow-on order for $5.1 million worth of Desert Hawk IIIs was made.

The Desert Hawk III incorporated many of the lessons learned during the initial deployment in Iraq, including lighter control and analysis stations, more reliable air vehicles and improved data links. The most obvious difference was that a more powerful engine allowed the air vehicle to be thrown into the air to launch it.

Hermes 450

In 2007 the Royal Artillery got its hands on the Hermes 450 tactical UAV to take over from the Phoenix. The new system represented a quantum leap in capabilities of several generations since the Phoenix was conceived in the mid 1980s. Advances in technology meant the Hermes 450 was dramatically more reliable and airworthy than the old Phoenix. The move to runway take-

The Hermes 450 tactical unmanned aerial vehicle has transformed the Royal Artillery's surveillance capabilities since it was introduced in 2007. (Thales)

off and landing dramatically improved the amount of fuel that could be carried to improve endurance and the size of sensors that it could carry. This also meant air vehicles endured far less stress and damage on landing so little maintenance and repair work was required to turn them around between missions.

The Hermes 450 had been in operational use for about 10 years when it was first leased by the UK in 2007, accumulating over 20,000 operational flight hours, mostly in combat service with the several air forces. So when the first deployed in Iraq in June 2007 there were few technical problems and the system's initial operational capability was declared on 5 July 2007

Unusually, the Hermes 450 were not bought outright by the UK Ministry of Defence but leased from UAV Tactical Systems Ltd (U-TacS), an inter-national partnership led by the UK arm of the French defence company Thales. The initial three year long contract worth approximately $110 million was activated in July 2007. It included training of the UK military personnel in use and maintenance of the system, and the provision of contractor logistic support (CLS) and programme management services. A follow-on eighteen-month contract worth $70 million was signed in October 2010.The Hermes 450's high wing and V-shaped tail optimizes aerodynamic and mission performance, because it gives the sensor turret a 360-degree performance. The air vehicle weighs 450kg on take-off, and is capable of carrying up to 150kg of internal and external payloads. Sensors on some versions include thermal imaging cameras, synthetic aperture radar and electronic surveillance equipment, but the British Army's variants were fitted only with cameras.

The aerodynamic performance of the Hermes 450 was also dramatically better than the old Phoenix. It could fly up to 16,000 feet and loiter at just over 110mph, meaning that people on the ground often had no idea it was watching them. A great enhancement had also been made in the perform-ance of data links since the 1980s and the Hermes operate 150 kilometres from the ground control station. This meant that all of south-eastern Iraq could be covered from a system based at Basra airbase. The sixteen-hour endurance of the air vehicle increased by more than four times the length of time the Hermes 450 could remain on station compared with the old Phoenix. This was a critical improvement over the old Phoenix and meant for the first time the Royal Artillery could carry out persistent surveillance of targets for days at a time, effectively allowing a Hermes 450 to be 'parked in orbit' over key parts of the battlefield.

Hermes 450

Wingspan:	10.5m
Fuselage length:	6.1m
Take-off weight:	450kg

Maximum usable fuel:	105kg
Maximum payload weight:	150kg
Payload power available:	1.6kW
Total engine power:	52hp @ 8,000RPM
Maximum mission radius:	200km
Maximum endurance:	16 hours
Operational altitude:	18,000ft
Maximum speed:	95 knots
Cruise speed:	70 knots
Stall speed:	42 knots
Maximum rate of climb:	500fpm

Major advances had also taken place in the performance of thermal imaging cameras since the 1980s and those on the Hermes 450 provided sufficient clarity and magnification to allow the type of small arms used by troops or insurgents on the ground to be identified.

The performance and reliability of the Hermes 450 was not only a major improvement on previous systems but the new UAV for the first time gave the British Army the ability to transmit live imagery from a UAV into remote receiving terminals used by forward air controllers and other ground units. Initially, the Hermes 450 could only transmit video imagery to bespoke terminals specific to the UAV but by the end of 2007 the Royal Artillery's UAVs had been modified to allow video imagery to be transmitted to the L-3 Communication ROVER terminals. These terminals were truly universal and could receive imagery from multiple sources, including aircraft, UAVs and helicopters equipped with compatible data links. This capability proved to be a major advance and ensured that the British Army had at last entered the era of twenty-first century network warfare.

Chapter 3

British Army in the Air –
The First Century

British soldiers first took to the skies in 1878 when tethered observation gas-filled balloons were purchased by the War Office to equip the Corps of Royal Engineers with the means to look over hills. In modern military jargon, this was a classic intelligence, surveillance, targeting acquisition and reconnaissance or ISTAR mission and centred around finding targets for the new generation of long-range howitzers being purchased for the Royal Artillery. These very basic balloons saw service in colonial campaigns and were eventually augmented by kites purchased from the America showman and aviation pioneer, Samuel Franklin Cody. He was soon hired as the Army's Kite Instructor at the army balloon school on the site of Farnborough airfield. He was also asked to set up two kite sections of the Royal Engineers and these later became the nucleus of the Air Battalion, Royal Engineers, which in turn became No. 1 Squadron, Royal Flying Corps and finally No. 1 Squadron, Royal Air Force.

After the Wright brothers made the first manned, powered flight in 1903, Cody started to build a machine similar to the famous Wright flier. He soon become the first man in the UK to build and fly his own powered aeroplane at the Army's first airfield at Farnborough on 16 October 1908, by flying a distance of more than 423 metres (463 yards, about a quarter of a mile). The next decade was a period of rapid advances in aviation and a few army officers and other well-to-do gentlemen purchased their own machines. In 1910 these gentlemen fliers managed to persuade the War Office to buy the army's first aircraft for observation and reconnaissance duties. The training of army pilots began at Larkhill and Netheravon was established as the first operational army airfield for troops manoeuvring on Salisbury Plain, and Upavon was opened as The Central Avery Flying School. The balloon and kite sections and companies of the Royal Engineers were now joined by the aeroplanes and it was decided to create an air battalion.

On 13 May 1912, the Royal Flying Corps (RFC) was born. Over the next six years the RFC and the aeroplane became a vital part of the battlefield scene. Communications, observation and reconnaissance, artillery gunfire control, air-to-air combat and bombing were all pioneered by the army fliers during the First World War.

The decision was taken to form the world's first independent air arm and on 1 April 1918, the Royal Air Force (RAF) came into existence and the army lost all of its aviation capability at a stroke. It was agreed that there would be Army Cooperation Squadrons, within the RAF, to assist with the specialist tasks such as observation and reconnaissance and artillery gunfire control.

This was a period of major defence budget cuts and army aviation stagnated until the late 1930s when the British Army began expanding as the prospect of war with Nazi Germany grew. The Royal Artillery petitioned for and acquired its own integral aviation support. The RAF was reluctant to allow the Army to have its own aircraft and the Army did not have the technical means to support them anyway, so a compromise was the formation

3-1 During the 1960s and 1970s, the Scout AH.1 was the AAC's workhorse at home and abroad. (Tim Ripley)

of the Air Observation Post (AOP) Squadrons. The Army commanded and controlled them and the RAF supplied and maintained the aircraft. Teams of RAF fitters worked under Royal Artillery commanding officers and pilots. This proved to be a highly successful arrangement and a series of new squadrons were formed. They operated in all theatres throughout the war.

After the formation of Britain's airborne forces in 1941 it was then decided to augment them with gliders to carry troops and heavy cargo, leading to the formation of the Glider Pilot Regiment (GPR) to fly them. The GPR played a major role in every operation of World War II, and elements also took part in the Burma campaign. In 1942, an Army Air Corps (AAC) was created to administer this newly formed Airborne Division but this was disbanded at the end of the war.

After World War II, the conscripts of wartime returned to civilian life. The AOP squadrons were reduced in number and the GPR reduced to just one squadron. Gliders were no longer required as a means of transport so the

The Lynx and Gazelle combination was the mainstay of AAC anti-tank operations in Germany during the Cold War. (Tim Ripley)

Massed formations of Lynx AH.7s were thought to be a key way to concentrate firepower to defeat Soviet armoured columns. (Private collection)

surviving members of the GPR carried out liaison and reconnaissance and observation duties as Light Liaison Flights alongside their AOP counterparts.

The 1950s saw the first combat use of helicopters and in 1955, the Joint Experimental Helicopter Unit (JEHU) was formed at Middle Wallop and was proved highly successful in providing integral support to the Army. The following year a Support Helicopter Flight from the JEHU would be deployed to Cyprus to assist the British Military in defeating the EOKA insurgent group. In 1956 all of the JEHU deployed on board HMS *Ocean* to the eastern Mediterranean to carry out the first amphibious airborne assault by ferrying Royal Marines to the dockside at El Gamil during the Suez crisis.

The value of the helicopter was proven by the Army and it was decided that the Army's aviation assets, in the form of the remaining AOP and GPR elements with their Auster 9 aeroplanes, should be reformed into what is today's Army Air Corps. On 1 September 1957 the AAC joined the order of battle of the Army with the primary roles of providing support in the form of observation and reconnaissance, artillery fire control, limited movement of men and materials and liaison. A number of additional roles soon evolved such as forward air control and radio relay.

During the 1960s, the AAC had expanded considerably and various flights spread throughout the Army, operating a mix of Westland Scout, Sud-Aviation Alouette 2 and Bell 47 Sioux light observation helicopters, supported

The TOW wire-guided missile armed Lynx AH.7 was the first AAC helicopter to possess effective long-range tank killing firepower. (Private collection)

by de Havilland Beaver light aircraft. It was then decided to streamline this organization and centralize the flights into brigade squadrons within divisional regiments. The World War II AOP Squadron numbers were dusted off and the beginnings of the present AAC regimental system took shape. Each division in the British Army had an AAC regiment and there were also several other flights providing support to other specialist organizations or remote locations.

The 1970s saw the AAC acquire the Westland Lynx helicopter, which was soon armed with the American-made TOW wire-guided anti-tank missile to turn it into an airborne tank killer. Although the Scout had been armed with French-made anti-tank missiles, the TOW was the first AAC weapon to be acquired in large enough numbers to allow a critical mass of combat helicopters to be fielded. The armed Lynx was teamed with the Westland

43

Gazelle, which was to scout ahead for targets. In the early 1980s, the Lynx-Gazelle combination was firmly established and every British division in Germany was supported by its own AAC anti-tank force.

During the mid-1980s, the newly formed 6 Airmobile Brigade in effect became the anti-tank reserve of the British Army of the Rhine (BAOR) in Germany. At the heart of British Army air mobile thinking at the time was the use of helicopters to react to Soviet armoured thrusts by rapidly deploying anti-tank missile firepower to set up blocking positions. In a series of exercises 6 Airmobile Brigade tested the concept of setting up 'killing zones' of helicopter-borne infantry missile teams and TOW missile-armed Lynx helicopters to blunt Soviet tank spearheads. Unlike the Americans, the British at this point did not envisage using their helicopters to 'fight through' enemy air defences to strike high value targets behind enemy lines. At this time the bulk of British military helicopters were not equipped with defensive systems or the long-range radios to allow them to fly beyond what was termed the 'forward line of troops' or FLOT into enemy-controlled air space let alone conduct deep strike missions.

Northern Ireland was a major commitment for the AAC from the 1970s to the early years of the twenty-first century. (Private collection)

The Lynx AH.9s bought in the late 1980s proved the usefulness of the helicopter in the light utility role. (Westland Helicopters)

6 Airmobile Brigade's concept of operations involved it deploying to a reserve position behind the main BAOR defensive line. Once the Soviet main effort of attack had been identified, reconnaissance teams would deploy by helicopter to scout out the best place to set up the main 6 Brigade blocking position. Then RAF Chinooks and Pumas would fly in the main infantry battalions, which each had forty-two Milan wire-guided missile teams assigned to them, to prepare defensive positions. To stand any chance of survival from Soviet artillery fire, the air mobile infantry battalions needed at least twenty-four hours in their positions to allow them to dig firing trenches with overhead protection. The brigade's main infantry fighting position was intended to be sited on ridge lines to give the Milan teams good fields of fire. It also meant the Lynx helicopter crews could use the high ground to shield them from view. They could then pop up from behind cover to join the missile barrage against the Soviet tank armada. Not surprisingly,

the employment of 6 Brigade was considered a 'one-shot' weapon. Once it was in position on the battlefield, its missile teams had limited mobility and when battle was joined with a Soviet tank force, British Army commanders clearly expected the brigade to go down fighting to buy time for heavy armoured forces to mass and mount an effective counter-attack and drive back the Soviets. The brigade was jokingly called a 'speed bump' for Red Army tanks. Even with its obvious limitations, the air mobile experiment was judged a success and in 1988 the airmobile brigade became a permanent feature of the British Army order of battle. A brigade based at Catterick in North Yorkshire was converted as a permanent air mobile formation.

From the 1970s and through until 2005, the British Army was heavily committed to the internal security campaign in Northern Ireland. The AAC played a major role in this effort and every one of its squadrons spent long months on tours in 'the province' over the years. This involved a mix of

UN duty in the Balkans in the mid-1990s pointed a way forward for the AAC to become involved in British Army expeditionary operations. (Tim Ripley)

The quality of the AAC's personnel – both air and ground crews – has always been its strong point. (Tim Ripley)

The success of the US Army AH-64A Apache in the 1991 Gulf War was instrumental in opening the way for the AAC to buy the potent attack helicopter. (US Army)

activities ranging from the classic liaison role flying senior commanders around Northern Ireland, to surveillance missions involving for the first time the use of airborne close-circuit television or heli-telly to observe the movement of ground troops in high threat areas, including the infamous bandit country of South Armagh. During its operations in South Armagh, AAC helicopters were damaged by Provisional IRA mortar attacks on British Army bases. On several occasions AAC helicopter crews found themselves in 'machine gun duels' with Provisional IRA gunners mounted on the back of trucks. There were persistent intelligence reports that the enemy had acquired heat-seeking shoulder-launched or Manpad anti-aircraft missiles, requiring AAC helicopters to be fitted for the first time with defensive equipment, including decoy flare dispensers and missile warning alarms.

The Iraqi invasion of Kuwait in August 1990 and the subsequent massing of Coalition forces in Saudi Arabia led to the largest deployment of British military helicopters to date. The AAC sent a full anti-tank regiment to be an offensive element of 1 (UK) Armoured Division to Saudi Arabia. 4 Regiment AAC, with 654, 659 and 661 Squadron attached, took twenty-four Lynx AH.7 TOW missile-armed helicopters and twenty-four Westland Gazelle AH.1 reconnaissance helicopters.

The regiment was assigned to the British division's offensive support group, which brought together its Royal Armoured Corps reconnaissance regiment, artillery regiments, and target-locating and army aviation assets into a single organization. Its mission was to find Iraqi tank concentrations and then rapidly bring overwhelming firepower down on the enemy positions. Operating in the first wave of British troops to advance into Iraq were 4 Regiment's armed reconnaissance patrols of Lynx and Gazelle helicopters. They worked closely with ground reconnaissance units during the so-called '100-hour war', as the drive by coalition ground troops into Kuwait and southern Iraq, was dubbed.

A handful of anti-tank engagements were conducted by 4 Regiment AAC in support of 1 (UK) Division's advance into southern Iraq, but heavy rain and low cloud severely hindered its operations. The first ever engagement by a British TOW-armed helicopter occurred on 26 February 1991, when Lynx of 654 Squadron AAC supporting 7 Armoured Brigade's attack on Objective Platinum destroyed two MTLB-armoured personnel carriers and four T-55 tanks with TOW missiles.

The end of the Cold War and the dramatic performance of US Army McDonnell Douglas (now Boeing) AH-64A Apache attack helicopters during

From the 1970s to the 1991 Gulf War the Midge drone was the only unmanned system in Royal Artillery service. (Tim Ripley)

deep attack missions during the 1991 Gulf War set in train a revolution of British Army thinking about air mobile operations.

US Army Apache destroyed approximately 500 Iraq tanks, 120 artillery pieces, 120 armoured personnel carriers, 300 trucks and 30 air defence sites during Operation Desert Storm, which convinced the British Army that it needed a similar capability. In the early summer of 1991, the United Kingdom Ministry of Defence formally endorsed Staff Target (Air) 428 for an attack helicopter, which set in train the procurement process that eventually led to the purchasing of Britain's Apache helicopters.

These were still primarily seen as anti-tank weapons and a major element of the case for buying the helicopters was a study in the late 1980s into the British Army's anti-tank weapon mix. The British had first been exposed to the US Army Apache during the late 1980s during NATO exercises and were hugely impressed by the night attack capabilities with the laser-guided Hellfire missile. This, however, at the time was not enough to shift spending priorities in the British Army during the mid-1980s. During this period, the British Army placed major orders for new tanks, armoured vehicles and self-propelled artillery. There were no major orders for new battlefield helicopters in the 1980s, except for the purchase of twenty-four unarmed utility Lynx AH.9s for 24 Airmobile Brigade, which took over the air mobile role from 6 Brigade in 1988.

Two years later an invitation to tender was issued, sparking a competition between the world's helicopter manufacturers for the prize of supplying ninety-one advanced attack helicopters to the British Army. For budgetary reasons the size of the purchase was later reduced to sixty-seven helicopters.

McDonnell Douglas offered its AH-64D version fitted with the Martin-Marrietta (now Lockheed Martin's Orlando business unit) Longbow milli-metre wave radar that allowed it to detect targets in rain and bad weather. The helicopters were to be assembled by Britain's only helicopter company, the then GKN subsidiary GKN-Westland Helicopters Ltd of Yeovil (now Italian-owned AgustaWestland). Bell Helicopters Textron teamed with GEC-Marconi to propose a British-built version of the AH-1W Cobra gunship then in service with the US Marine Corps, with the UK-assembled version dubbed the Cobra Venom. British Aerospace (now BAE Systems) and Eurocopter joined forces to offer the Tiger gunship. South Africa's Denel entered the fray teamed with Marshalls of Cambridge to offer the Kestrel/Rooivalk gunship. Italy's Agusta offered its A129 Mangusta and the Boeing/Sikorsky team put their RAH-66 Comanche into the fray. An outsider that never got formally into the contest was the Russian Kamov Ka-50.

The contest was noted for high-profile sales stunts and over-the-top lobbying but it was clear that the British Army only wanted the Apache and some observers suggested that the staff requirement was actually written in such a way that the Apache was bound to win. For example, only the Apache boasted the adverse weather attack capability offered by its millimetre wave radar. The inclusion of Rolls-Royce in the Westland-McDonnell Douglas team was also an astute move because the company's lobbying power is renowned in Whitehall, particularly within both the Ministry of Defence and the then Department for Trade and Industry.

In one of his first acts after being appointed UK Defence Secretary, Michael Portillo oversaw the selection of the Apache in July 1995 and the contracting of the deal in April 1996. Westland Helicopters won the prime contract to deliver sixty-seven helicopters, and Rolls-Royce was selected to supply the engines for them, giving the deal a high 'made in Britain' content. The programme was now no longer an 'off the shelf' purchase and this would impact at a later date as the contractors ran into problems developing and delivering many of its complex 'UK only' elements.

The first order for the Phoenix unmanned aerial vehicle was placed in the mid-1980s but technical problems would delay its entry to service by a decade. (Tim Ripley)

The early 1990s was a period of major upheaval in the British Army as it coped with the aftermath of the collapse of the Berlin Wall and the end of the Cold War. UK defence spending was cut back, while the defence budget and the size of the Army were both cut by a third. This culminated in the 1992 Options for Change defence spending cuts programme, which envisaged a major withdrawal of British forces from Germany and the establishment of what was termed a 'capability-based' armed forces. No longer would the British military be specifically tailored to solely fight the Red Army but would have to field a range of generic capabilities to enable it to deal with a variety of potential opponents and scenarios, known as 'contingent operations'. Direct threats to the UK homeland or our major NATO allies were declared to be minimal and future operations would have to deal with incidents far from home.

For the AAC it brought mixed news. Its place in the British Army's order of battle was confirmed and it was envisaged that it would eventually take control of the Apache force. At the same time, the role of 24 Airmobile Brigade was to be transformed into a more wide-ranging formation capable of projecting its fighting troops by air over some 120 kilometres at short notice. The anti-tank 'speed bump' concept was history and the British Army's air mobile force was now considered an offensive capability.

At the heart of air manoeuvre developments during the 1990s was the concept of the aviation battlegroup, which envisaged an AAC regiment operating as an independent force on the battlefield with a range of other arms, including infantry, ground reconnaissance artillery and engineer units under its command. The concept revolved around the aviation battlegroup being given responsibility for specific areas of terrain to occupy or dominate with helicopters patrols and indirect artillery fire.

During the British involvement in the Bosnian civil war during the 1990s, the AAC dispatched many of its regiments and squadrons to serve under the United Nations and subsequently NATO direction. A detachment of 664 Squadron deployed to support the UN in the spring of 1995 and 3 Regiment was assigned to the UN Rapid Reaction Force, as part of 24 Brigade, later that year. The regiment, however, was not called into action before the war ended and NATO peace enforcement troops deployed in December 1995. Spearheading the British participation in NATO mission was 1 Regiment AAC, which deployed in full strength to patrol the ethnic flash points of north-west Bosnia. It came within minutes of engaging Bosnian tanks on one occasion but otherwise did not fire a shot in anger.

Unfortunately, the British Army's ambitious plans for 24 Brigade were not matched by the required level of funding. The Apache were not actually ordered until 1996 and they would not be scheduled to enter service for another five years.

Army Air Corps Order of Battle, 2000

Unit	Base	Type	Role
UK BASED UNITS			
HQ Director Army Aviation	Middle Wallop, Hampshire		
667 Squadron		Westland Lynx AH.7, Westland Gazelle AH.1	Development & trials
651 Squadron (forming)		AgustaWestland Apache AH.1	Development & trials
Army Historic Aircraft Flight		Auster AOP.9, DHC 1 Chipmunk T.10, de Havilland Beaver AL.1, Sud Alouette AH.2, Westland Scout AH.1, Bell Sioux AH.1, Saunders-Roe Skeeter AOP.12	Display flying
School of Army Aviation 2 Regiment	Middle Wallop, Hampshire		
670 Squadron		Eurocopter Squirrel HT.2	Advanced rotary-wing training
671 Squadron		Westland Lynx AH.7, Westland Gazelle AH.1, Bell 212HP AH.1	Operational training
ATS		Westland Gazelle AH.1	Aircrewman training
660 Squadron/DHFS	RAF Shawbury, Shropshire	Eurocopter Squirrel HT.1	Basic rotary-wing training
674 Squadron***	RAF Barkston Heath, Lincolnshire, Middle Wallop, Hampshire	Slingsby T.67M Firefly 260	Primary training
Advanced Fixed Wing Flight	Middle Wallop, Hampshire	Britten-Norman Islander AL.1	Utility/Liaison/ Observation
3 Regiment	Wattisham, Suffolk		
653 Squadron		Westland Lynx AH.9	Utility
662 Squadron		Westland Lynx AH.7/ Gazelle AH.1	Anti tank
663 Squadron		Westland Lynx AH.7/ Gazelle AH.1	Anti tank
4 Regiment	Wattisham, Suffolk		
654 Squadron		Westland Lynx AH.7/ Gazelle AH.1	Anti tank
659 Squadron		Westland Lynx AH.9	Utility
669 Squadron		Westland Lynx AH.7/ Gazelle AH.1	Anti tank
5 Regiment	Aldergrove, Northern Ireland		
665 Squadron		Westland Gazelle AH.1	Observation
655 Squadron		Westland Lynx AH.7	Observation/ Utility
1 Flight		Britten-Norman Islander AL.1	Utility/Liaison/ Observation

Unit	Base	Type	Role
7 Regiment (V) (TA) Regiment	Netheravon		
658 Squadron (V)		Westland Gazelle AH.1	Observation
666 Squadron (V)		Westland Gazelle AH.1	Observation
3 Flight (V)	RAF Leuchars	Westland Gazelle AH.1	Observation
6 Flight (V)	RAF Shawbury	Westland Gazelle AH.1	Observation
9 Regiment	Dishforth, North Yorkshire		
656 Squadron		Westland Lynx AH.7/ Gazelle AH.1	Anti tank
657 Squadron (to Odiham 2001 for SF Support)		Westland Lynx AH.7/ Gazelle AH.1	Anti tank
664 Squadron		Westland Lynx AH.7/ Gazelle AH.1	Anti tank
672 Squadron (forming)		Westland Lynx AH.7/ Gazelle AH.1	Anti-tank
Independent Units			
8 Flight Hereford		Westland Gazelle AH.1.A109A	SF Support
GERMANY			
1 Regiment	Gütersloh, Germany		
651 Squadron (to be AH Fielding Sqn in UK 2001)		Westland Lynx AH.7/ Gazelle AH.1	Anti tank
652 Squadron		Westland Lynx AH.7/ Gazelle AH.1	Anti tank
661 Squadron		Westland Lynx AH.7/ Gazelle AH.1	Anti tank
OTHER OVERSEAS BASED UNITS			
7 Flight	Seria, Brunei	Bell 212HP AH.1	Training Support
12 Flight	RAF Bruggan	Westland Gazelle AH.1	HQ ARRC Support
16 Flight	Dhekalia, Cyprus	Westland Gazelle AH.1	Training Support
25 Flight	Belize City, Belize	Westland Gazelle AH.1	Training Support
29 (BATUS) Flight	Suffield, Canada	Westland Gazelle AH.1	Training Support

Notes:
*** 674 Squadron is part of No. 1 Elementary Flying Training School at RAF Barkston Heath (with a Middle Wallop detachment).

Key:

AHTU	Advanced Helicopter Training Unit
ATS	Aircrewman Training Squadron
BATUS	British Army Training Unit Suffield
DHFS	Defence Helicopter Flying School
V/TA	Volunteer/Territorial Army

The British Army's involvement with UAVs stretches back to the early 1960s when the Royal Artillery acquired American Northrop MQM-57 drones to spot targets for its nuclear warhead-armed rocket regiments. These early propeller-powered drones served from 1964 to 1972 in 57 (Bhurtpore) Battery of 94th Locating Regiment.

In June 1963, Canada and Britain agreed to evaluate the turbojet-powered Canadair CL-89 drone. The first complete CL-89 system was supplied to the West Germans in 1969. During the 1970s, both France and Italy joined the British and West Germans in operating the CL-89. NATO gave the system the designation AN/USD-501 and in UK service it was known as 'Midge'. The system was designed for information collecting at a divisional level.

The CL-89 drone system gathered data by flight over pre-planned flight paths using 'wet film' cameras and infra-red sensors, which meant any intelligence collected was always several hours' old by the time it could passed to commanders. Midge saw service with 94th Locating Regiment from 1972 for almost twenty years. The Midge was used operationally in Kuwait in 1991 but the fast moving ground war meant it made little contribution to the war.

Although the Lebanon war in the 1980s and the 1991 Gulf War saw extensive use of UAVs for intelligence, surveillance, targeting and surveillance (ISTAR) roles the British Army was not in the leading edge of military organizations experimenting with the new form of 'eye-in-the-sky'. Almost all its budget for surveillance was tied up in the Phoenix programme for most of the 1990s. Technical glitches led to delays and by the time the Phoenix entered service in 1998 its cost had escalated to nearly £300 million making it one of the most notorious defence equipment procurement scandals of the 1990s.

Full acceptance into service followed the completion of conversion training by the Royal Artillery's 22 Locating Battery, which was then part of 32nd Regiment and 57 Battery, which was part of 39th Regiment. Both regiments are equipped with the Multiple-Launch Rocket System (MLRS) in the depth-fire role, supporting 3 (UK) Division in the southern England and 1 (UK) Armoured Division in Germany, respectively. The Phoenix was still primarily in the target acquisition role to provide images and data for the two MLRS regiments and others artillery units equipped with AS90 155mm self-propelled howitzers.

The deployment of the Phoenix to Kosovo between 1999 and 2001 and the American experience of using UAVs in the Balkans and Afghanistan led to the British Army showing increasing interest in UAVs. It was decided to concentrate all the Royal Artillery's UAVs into a single regiment based on Salisbury Plain in Wiltshire. This saw 57 Battery move south to Larkhill from its old base in Northumberland to join 22 Battery as the new re-vamped 32nd Regiment alongside 18 Battery, which was also converted to the Phoenix role. 42 Battery joined 32nd Regiment in 2004 to give the British Army's only UAV unit four Phoenix batteries.

From 2003 to 2006, the Ministry of Defence launched the Joint UAV Experimentation Programme (JUEP) to explore the further potential of

UAVs and determine their utility both in the single and joint Service arena. This involved experiments on mini-UAVs, including the Lockheed Martin Desert Hawk and MiTex Buster. The biggest JUEP activity involved using leased Israeli Aircraft Industries Heron UAVs in Canada during a major armoured battlegroup training exercise.

Chapter 4

Phoenix over Kosovo, 1999 to 2001

In the gloom of the early evening a Kosovo hillside is a hive of activity. A team of British soldiers are hard at work preparing for the nightly launch of a Phoenix unmanned aerial vehicle (UAV). Dozens of local villagers have gathered to watch the proceedings. What these people, who only a few weeks before were hiding in the hills from Serb paramilitary forces, made of the strange goings-on of the Royal Artillery Phoenix launch detachment was hard to discern. But when the Phoenix flew off the rail into the night sky some clapped and cheered.

By late July 1999, Phoenix were being launched on regular night time missions to monitor the Kosovo-Serbia border for suspicious activity. This was only a few weeks after the first Phoenix battery had deployed to the Balkans at the height of the Operation Allied Force strategic air campaign and within days of arriving it was re-roled to support the move of NATO peacekeeping troops into Kosovo.

For the British Army the experience of using their Phoenix system in a real world operational deployment was something of an eye opener. Many lessons were learnt and Phoenix operators greatly improved their understanding of the system's capabilities and limitations. More importantly it opened up the debate in the Army and in the Royal Air Force over the role of UAVs in a wide range of possible scenarios.

Planning for the possible deployment of Phoenix to the Balkans began in the early spring of 1999 when British troops first began deploying to Macedonia, just prior to the start of the NATO air strikes on 24 March. 'When 4 Armoured Brigade came out then they identified a requirement to use us in the defence of Macedonia, in case of a concerted Serb attack or incursion,' a senior officer of the Royal Artillery's 22 Battery recalled. 'But the weather conditions – icing – prohibited us coming out.'

By May the RAF high command was getting increasingly frustrated that their BAe Harrier GR7 attack aircraft were finding it difficult to identify Serb

Phoenix unmanned aerial vehicles made their first flights over Kosovo to monitor the Yugoslav army withdrawal in June 1999. (KFOR)

tanks and artillery in woods and hills of Kosovo. More often than not the Harriers returned to their base in Italy without dropping their bombs.

'Things got going in mid-May when the RAF asked for us to assist in their targeting – they saw us as a pair of eyes to direct GR7 close air support' said the officer. 'The RAF needed UAVs because they had nothing that could fly [safely] below the cloud base [to find targets] – that drove our deployment.'

The idea was for a forward air controller to be based in the Phoenix ground control station (GCS) in Macedonia to use the UAV to find targets and then to direct Harriers to attack them.

This novel concept of operations was, however, perhaps too radical for the American leadership of the NATO air campaign. 'The American way is to receive information about a target and then task an airborne forward air controller (AFAC) to look at a target,' said the officer.

NATO rules of engagement also called for a second pair of eyes, either in an aircraft or via a UAV sensor, to identify the target for attack and then for the Combined Air Operations Centre, at Vicenza in Italy, which controlled all NATO air operations over Balkans, to clear the aircraft to attack. These stringent rules of engagement were instigated to limit instances of collateral damage on civilian targets. The idea of a RAF Harrier attacking a target on the basis of information from a British UAV, without an AFAC overhead or real-time link to the CAOC, did not find favour with the senior USAF generals in Vicenza.

'The problem was how to plumb the information from our GCS in Macedonia into the strategic air campaign,' commented one 22 Battery officer involved in this phase of the campaign. 'The real-time satellite link was not set up in time to the CAOC. I generated a statement of requirement. The satellite communications links would have required large bandwidth.'

The amount of bandwidth required was so extensive that British Ministry of Defence (MOD) communications experts believed UK-dedicated military satellite systems would be overloaded if they were used to transmit Phoenix video imagery. Existing communications needs had greater priority so investigations were made to transmit Phoenix imagery by hiring commercial bandwidth or piggy backing on the US Global Broadcast System (GBS), which was being used by US Army IAI/TRW Hunter UAVs already based in Macedonia.

Royal Artillery Phoenix launch teams moved into Kovoso behind NATO troops to keep Yugoslav forces under surveillance. (KFOR)

Intense discussions were also under way with the Macedonian government for an agreement to allow the Phoenix unit to operate from its territory. The Macedonians were very sensitive about offensive operations being conducted from their territory and the British agreed to seek their permission before conducting any targeting operations by Phoenix units based in the Balkan country.

As these problems were being assessed, the Kosovo conflict had reached its climax and by early June 1999 the Yugoslav leadership had agreed to a Finnish-Russian brokered peace plan.

So, by the time the battery and its 27 Phoenix air vehicles and support equipment had arrived in the Balkans by ship, the air campaign was effectively over with NATO ground troops about to enter Kosovo. The strategic environment had dramatically altered, and new plans were now required.

Monitoring ethnic tension between Serb and Albanians was the main role of the Phoenix once NATO troops had taken control of Kosovo. (KFOR)

Another important task of the Phoenix was monitoring the tense border of the province with Yugoslavia. (KFOR)

One 22 Battery officer recalled:

> We started operations right in the middle of the peace talks on 9th June and had flown more than 77 missions by the end of July. We flew a series of tasks into Kosovo up the main NATO entry routes. We recorded every flight in the GCS and then showed the video to people in the British 4 Brigade headquarters. This is our first operational deployment 'out of role' – Phoenix was designed for artillery fire direction – so the things we did here were not envisaged when the system was procured. It took a little time for the Brigade headquarters to understand how much Phoenix could offer them. They hadn't used us before. Then we couldn't pipe our video around different offices in the headquarters. We also produced written summaries or reports of our missions.

The UK Defence Evaluation Research Agency (DERA) conducted a feasibility study on piping Phoenix video imagery around headquarters through a fibre optic cable. Later in the summer of 1999, a limited capability was deployed to Kosovo to allow a 22 Battery data transmission terminal to flow video directly into 4 Brigade's headquarter complex. A similar package of transmission capabilities was subsequently developed to allow this to be done again on future operations.

'We flew ahead of the troops during the insertion operation, looking at options for the next phase rather than looking at what our troops were doing,' said one 22 Battery Phoenix operator. The Phoenix confirmed that Serb troops were, in fact, withdrawing from Kosovo and, in their biggest coup of the operation, filmed eleven Serb MiG-21 fighters roll out of deep tunnel shelters at Pristina airport on 11 June, prior to them taking off for Belgrade.

'When we first flew into Kosovo there was not a benign environment and two air vehicles were shot down,' said the operator. 'They were over Serb positions and all of a sudden we lost contact – we had no indication of a technical failure being imminent. One was lost before we entered Kosovo and one as we were monitoring the Serb withdrawal.'

Apparently, NATO senior commanders did not classify the later incident as a hostile act that breached the military technical agreement [between

Phoenix launch troops move around Kosovo to conduct missions where NATO commanders wanted. (Tim Ripley)

NATO and Serbs governing the withdrawal of Yugoslav troops] because there was a political imperative to get the Serb forces out of Kosovo. It seems there was also a feeling in NATO circles that because the Phoenix was unmanned, the Serbs were deemed not to be directly threatening allied troops. 'There was less concern because they were not trying to kill our people,' said one NATO officer.

However, the Phoenix battery took note of the vulnerability of their air vehicles and at the first opportunity started to fly them predominately at night.

22 Battery moved forward into Kosovo in mid-June to support NATO peacekeeping operations to bring security to the lawless province and this has provided different operational challenges.

'We now do tasking for Headquarters Kosovo Force (KFOR) and 4 Brigade,' said a 22 Battery officer in August 1999.

> We usually launched one air vehicle a day. We are told to go and look at a specific area, in order to detect activity that threatens the secure environment. It is important to remember the deterrent effect of people hearing the air vehicle flying overhead. We learnt this on experiments at the British Army Training Unit in Suffield Canada experiment in 1998.
>
> We launch the air vehicle from our forward operating base and then handed over to a GCS, which could pass information to 4 Brigade. It was important that we have the ability to cover all the Brigade's area of responsibility.

The tactical grouping of the battery for missions was unconventional, with two troops-worth of people deploying with three troops-worth of equipment. This allowed a spare GCS to be deployed to 4 Brigade and other allied headquarters to enable imagery to be distributed. It also gave a degree of redundancy to the battery's equipment inventory.

A 22 Battery officer recalled:

> Air space management was the big thing here in Kosovo. There were all the various allied UAV systems, more than a hundred helicopters, identification friend or foe systems and ground control issues all running in parallel with getting the international airport [at Pristina] operating again. Co-ordination was challenging – this is the biggest lesson from here. When I got back I sent my operations officer on a RAF air space managers course to learn all the procedures. This is our first experience of multi-national joint ops.

Complex air control measures had to be put in place over Kosovo to ensure Phoenix did not interfere with NATO military flights or civilian air traffic. (KFOR)

He continued:

> The battery had to become almost like the Army Air Corps – living and breathing air space management. We were initially based near Pristina but we had to move the launch and recovery set up to Podujevo because there were just too many helicopters around Pristina.

This meant the battery had to split itself between its battery command post and echelon based together, in a disused factory on the outskirts of Pristina, and the forward-operating location in the north of Kosovo.

The first phase of the Kosovo campaign threw up possible requirements for upgrades to the air vehicle, including more powerful engines for greater endurance and improved sensors, according to Royal Artillery Phoenix operators.

One other issue to emerge was the logistic support necessary to sustain the battery and it highlighted a possible need for lighter and smaller support vehicles. 'We have 27 air vehicles and 55 trucks – this was a deliberate operation,' said a 22 Battery planning officer. 'We were a logistic heavy operation – 46 people are involved in flying the air vehicles and the remainder of the 126 were in the battery in supporting roles.'

22 Battery returned to its home base on Salisbury Plain, in the UK, during late August. The battery's deployment to Kosovo had provided the British Army with the opportunity to use UAVs, with a real-time surveillance capability, in action for the first time. A succession of high-level visitors took the opportunity to drop in on the battery in Kosovo, indicating that interest in UAVs remains high in Britain.

22 Battery returned to Kosovo in May 2000, attached to 1st Regiment Royal Horse Artillery, and had flown more than 120 missions by early August. 'Our mission was to support KFOR's [Kosovo Force's] British-commanded Multi-National Brigade (Centre) – we were a key component of its surveillance and target acquisition capability,' said a 22 Battery officer. The unit's UAVs were tasked with patrolling the ground security zone on Kosovo's boundary with Serbia to ensure compliance, and with providing aerial support to the brigade's battle groups in Kosovo. He said:

> On receiving tasking, battlegroups send a liaison officer with com-
> munications [personnel] to sit in our ground control station and tell
> us where they want us to fly, [then] we give him three hours of
> thermal imaging in support of ground operations. As the liaison
> officer identifies trouble, he speaks on his radio to the quick-reaction
> force, deploying them to sites of interest [by ground or helicopter].

The UAV had been tasked by brigade personnel from Finland, Norway, Sweden and the UK, with the 22 Battery officer describing the battle groups as 'real fans' of the capability. The Phoenix was also routinely used at night as part of the brigade's integrated surveillance and patrolling plan. The air vehicles had been equipped with an airspace transponder with a global positioning system, an infra-red strobe to help recovery crews find them in rough terrain fields at night.

Describing the UAV as 'an eye opener', Brigadier Robert Fry, the commander of Multi-National Brigade (Centre), said that the system, in combination with manned and technical reconnaissance assets, delivered 'a degree of surveillance capability normally only found at divisional level'.

Phoenix were flying unprecedented combined missions with quick-reaction forces carried in UK RAF Westland Puma HC.1 support helicopters as part of the NATO peacekeeping mission. This was a first for the British armed forces, which are employing the Phoenix in the surveillance role to counter ethnic violence. During these missions a Phoenix, on task as part of a planned operation, would be used to co-ordinate the deployment by helicopter of a quick-reaction force of infantry to within 100m of a target detected by the UAV. A 22 Battery Phoenix operator, who described the joint effort as a great success, recalled:

> There was close detailed airspace co-ordination. It was useful to prove that UAVs and manual aircraft are not mutually exclusive in the same airspace, [and] were the key to convincing aircraft pilots that you can have manned and unmanned aircraft in the same airspace.

During 22 Battery's deployments the system flew around 270 missions and on 29 missions either the airframe and/or the sensor payload was lost or written off because of damage.

Phoenix, this time operated by 57 Battery of 39th Regiment Royal Artillery, returned to Kosovo in April 2001 for the third consecutive year as tension continued to be high between the Yugoslav province's Albanian and Serb populations.

Joint strike operations with NATO heli-borne quick reaction forces was a common mission for Phoenix in the later years of the NATO mission in Kosovo. (KFOR)

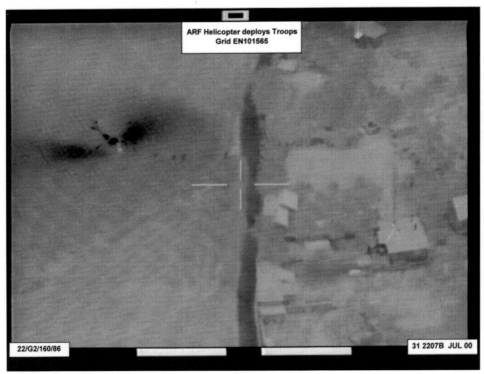

Phoenix was withdrawn from Kosovo in 2001 after three major deployments that demonstrated the systems capabilities to many senior British officers. (KFOR)

According to a 57 Battery's officer, between 20 April and 11 August 2001 the unit conducted 109 Phoenix flights, of which 79 were completely successful. He said seven air vehicles were destroyed during this period. The main role of the battery was to support KFOR patrols protecting the UN-administered province's Serb minorities from attack. 'We're doing ethnic protection, helping protect enclaves through deterrence,' said the officer. 'People won't leave houses when Phoenix is overhead – they think they are being watched and are wary of it.'

Phoenix was not used to support Operation Eagle, the NATO interdiction effort along the Macedonia-Kosovo border to prevent Albanian insurgents join the civil war in the neighbouring country, because the high mountain peaks in the region were above the UAV's flight ceiling. 57 Battery also deployed to the US sector of Kosovo to help monitor the return of Yugoslav police and army units in the ground security zone along the province's boundary with Serbia.

By the summer of 2001, plans were at an advanced stage for the British Army to concentrate its operational UAV activities under the control of a single regiment, based at Larkhill, England. This eventually saw 57 Battery based near Newcastle-upon-Tyne in north-east England, joining 22 Battery in 32nd Regiment at Larkhill, Wiltshire. 'The idea is to bring together the two batteries so we can concentrate the BAE Systems contractor logistic support and reduce a lot of duplication,' said an officer assigned to 57 Battery during its deployment with KFOR. The move would also concentrate the Army's growing experience of UAV operations and signified that the Phoenix was now considered to be more than just an artillery target location system.

Chapter 5

Lynx and Gazelle Support NATO in Kosovo, 1999 to 2001

From a few hundred feet above the road into Kosovo could be seen to be jammed with green-painted tanks, armoured vehicles, trucks and Land Rovers. In the fields in either side of the road the crew of the 659 Squadron Army Air Corps (AAC) Westland Lynx AH.9 could see thousands of Kosovar Albanian refugees cheering on 4 Armoured Brigade's soldiers as they moved into the Kacanik gorge to begin the liberation of their home land.

In the back of the helicopter, Brigadier Adrian Freer, the commander of 5 Airborne Brigade, was listening into the multiple radio nets as he choreographed his troops who had the key job of securing the gorge, ahead of the advance by 4 Brigade. At key moments in the operation, the Brigadier ordered the helicopter's pilot to put him down on the road into Kosovo so he could hold impromptu meetings with British commanders responsible for keeping traffic moving along the gorge that connected Macedonia with the Yugoslav province of Kosovo.

Later in the day, Major Richard Leakey, 659 Squadron's boss, led a pair of Lynx carrying NATO's senior commander, Lieutenant General Mike Jackson, and his senior staff into Kosovo to hold a press conference outside Pristina airport, which had been controversially occupied by Russian troops. As General Jackson's Lynx crossed the border, a heavy rain storm broke over southern Kosovo and Major Leakey had to land the helicopter until the weather cleared. He put the Lynx down next to a detachment of British troops who had just liberated a petrol filling station beside the main road to the capital of Kosovo, Pristina. After a brief cup of tea, the weather cleared and the helicopters took off for the brief flight to the airport. The arrival of the helicopters was broadcast live on global rolling news channels, putting the Army Air Corps (AAC) well and truly in the global eye.

For Leakey and his squadron, the operation to move NATO troops into Kosovo was the high point of their seven month-long tour to the Balkans. When they arrived in Macedonia in the freezing cold of February, only a few hundred NATO troops were on the ground preparing to move into Kosovo to help manage a peace deal between Albanian and Serb leaders that was being brokered by international mediators. It was hoped that the deal would end several months of bloody fighting between Albanian guerrilla fighters and Yugoslav forces, which had forced tens of thousands of civilians to flee their homes. Ethnic hatred ran deep between the majority Albanian population of Kosovo and the Serbs, who regarded the province as their cultural and historical heartland.

NATO deployed its Allied Rapid Reaction Corps (ARRC) Headquarters to neighbouring Macedonia to act as the co-ordinating command for any peacekeeping force that might be deployed to keep the two sides apart. The British-led ARRC Headquarters was commanded by General Jackson and he took with him his own flight of Lynx helicopters to give him the ability to move quickly around the theatre of operations. This was a classic 'taxi-cab'

Macedonia's Petrovec airport became home of AAC Lynx AH.9 helicopters of 659 Squadron AAC in February 1999. (KFOR)

Transporting senior NATO military and diplomatic figures around Kosovo, Macedonia and Albania was at the centre of 659 Squadron's role. (Tim Ripley)

mission that had been the bread and butter of the AAC since its formation in 1957 but the complex and fast-moving nature of the Kosovo crisis meant that 659 Squadron was at the centre of global events. The NATO air campaign meant that 659 Squadron's Lynx had to be fitted with cutting-edge technology to ensure its pilots could talk to other alliance aircraft and avoid being mistaken for Serb helicopters.

Leakey recalled:

> We were the command flight – we provided helicopters to support General Jackson and his staff. We also flew any VIPs who came to visit as the crisis escalated – we flew Prime Minister Tony Blair, Defence Secretary George Robertson, UN Mission in Kosovo chief Bernard Kouchner and US Army General Wesley Clark, NATO's Supreme Allied Commander Europe (SACEUR).
>
> We arrived in February in the back of a giant Russian Antonov An-124 airlifter. We had three aircraft at first but I wanted to have two aircraft up whenever we were flying VIPs so we asked for and got a fourth aircraft.

71

Given the importance of the mission and the high profile of the passengers to be carried, Leakey's helicopters received secure radio systems and enhanced identification friend of foe (IFF) devices. Leakey said:

> The IFF situation was a significant factor in what ever we did. We had Mode 1,2,3,4, to allow the NATO Boeing E-3A Sentry AWAC radar aircraft to see us. We were all very conscious about F-15-Blackhawk shoot-down type incidents.

The 659 Squadron detachment set up base at the side of the runway at Macedonia's main civil airport, a fifteen-minute drive to the east of the country's capital Skopje, where General Jackson had his headquarters. Along the flight line at Petrovec airport were the ageing Mil Mi-8 HIP helicopters of the Macedonian air force and the second-hand McDonnell Douglas DC-9 airliners of the state airline MAT.

'We were some of the first British troops in theatre and at the time it was a pretty benign environment in Macedonia,' Leakey said. 'We expected to

Giant Russian Antonov An-124 transport aircraft were leased to fly 659 Squadron's four helicopters to Macedonia. (KFOR)

The use of Russian Antonov An-124s would become a very common feature of AAC
deployments in the Balkans, Middle East and Afghanistan over the next decade.
(KFOR)

Albanian refugees flooded into Macedonia in March 1999 and NATO forces rushed to help build refugee camps for them. (KFOR)

659 Squadron's Lynx were used to bypass traffic chaos and deliver humanitarian aid to refugee camps. (KFOR)

quickly enter Kosovo in the wake of the Rambouillet peace talks that were then under way in France.'

The talks broke down amid acrimony and the Yugoslav strongman President Slobodan Milosevic then refused to heed an ultimatum from NATO. On 24 March, NATO aircraft started bombing targets throughout Yugoslavia to try to coerce the Serbs to return to peace talks.

Leakey recalled:

When the NATO bombing campaign started there was a significant threat of Yugoslav special force, artillery, air strikes and helicopter raids on Petrovec airport. This was the assessment of the intelligence guys and we took it very seriously. We dug air raid shelters and were filmed by Sky TV diving into them. We thought NATO's helicopters at Petrovec would be the target of any raids.

Macedonia's majority Orthodox population were far from happy that NATO was bombing Yugoslavia and there were several days of rioting in Skopje and a 659 Squadron Lynx was caught up in one of these riots. 'We had an aircraft downtown trying to land the US-peace envoy Ambassador William Walker, when it was attacked by a stone-throwing mob,' said Leakey.

Milosevic reacted to type and unleashed hundreds of paramilitary thugs to intimidate the Albanian population to flee their homes. Hundreds of

The NATO insertion operation in Kosovo, June 1999. (NATO)

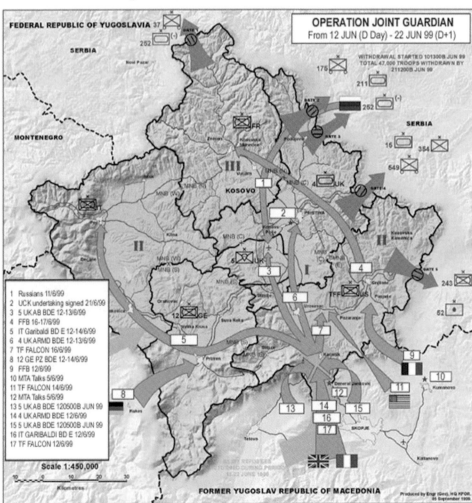

AAC Lynx had to share the ramp and runway at Petrovec airport with civil traffic. (KFOR)

thousands were forced to walk to the borders with Albania and Macedonia, or crowded on trains that rolled south to deposit them at Kacanik.

The Macedonian government and international aid agencies were overwhelmed by the torrent of starving and traumatized refugees that were pouring through the Kacanik border crossing. Many just set up camp in the fields on either side of the road and tried to find some sort of shelter from the freezing Balkan winter.

Seeing the crisis unfolding, General Jackson ordered his troops to take the lead and try to set up refugee camps, as well as organizing sanitation and feeding. An international airlift of aid was started into Petrovec airport but there were not enough trucks to get the precious cargo out to the makeshift refugee camps to the north of Skopje.

Leakey continues:

> All the aid was coming into Skopje airport in the back of C-130s. I offered up the squadron to lift the stuff in underslung loads and the General said OK. We were the first helicopters to fly aid to the refugee camps. We took in 5,000 blankets, 5000kg of baby milk, water and medicine. Once the situation stabilized we were able to stand down and reverted to our main role and then started flying VIP visitors to the refugee centres.

By June, the Yugoslavs had been enduring almost three months of NATO bombing, the US and Britain were hinting that they might commit ground troops and Milosevic's Russian allies appeared to be on the verge of withdrawing crucial diplomatic support. Milosevic agreed to peace talks and then signed up to an international plan to allow NATO peacekeeping troops to enter Kosovo to monitor the withdrawal of Yugoslav regular troops and Serb paramilitary forces. General Jackson had several tense meetings with the Yugoslav military high command to agree the terms of the withdrawal and entry of NATO's Kosovo Force (KFOR). Dawn on 12 June was set for the arrangements to come into effect.

For 659 Squadron, the pace of life suddenly quickened. British troops from 5 Airborne and 4 Armoured Brigades would spearhead the drive up the Kacanik gorge to open the road to Pristina.

'On 12th June we had one aircraft with 5 Brigade from 4.30 a.m., flying its commander around,' said Leakey. 'Then the aircraft was tasked to lift explosive ordnance disposal and engineer teams to do route clearance on the tunnels and bridges in the Kacanik define. Another aircraft was at the head of Route Hawk doing route clearance.'

As the operation to move into Kosovo was unfolding it was emerging that 300 Russian troops had driven down from Bosnia, through Serbia, to Pristina and then on to its airport. The arrival of the Russians, who were not under General Jackson's command, was a major complicating factor that threatened to unravel the withdrawal agreements he had brokered with the Yugoslavs. Famously, General Clark had initially order General Jackson to evict the Russians by force but the British commander had ignored the orders. It was now time to come to an accommodation with the Russians so the operation could proceed to plan.

Leakey said:

> In the afternoon two aircraft flew up to Pristina airfield with General Jackson for his press conference in the rain. I flew him. It was quite exciting because we were very uncertain of the role of the Russians. How would they respond? It was an uncertain atmosphere. I never felt under threat or under a direct menacing attitude. The eyes of the world were on us.

Over the next week the Yugoslav withdrawal was successfully completed and NATO peacekeeping troops moved to take full control of Kosovo to allow UN and other aid agencies to help the refugees return home.

'Our mission did not change once we were in Kosovo,' said Leakey. 'We continued to fly the General and other VIPs to the main centres and bases in Kosovo.'

659 Squadron moved to establish a forward operating base (FOB) at General Jackson's headquarters on the outskirts of Pristina. In the first few weeks of the NATO mission, the FOB at the Film City Headquarters was little more than a few tents in a field. It grew to include a command post, operations and intelligence cells, an aircrew briefing facility, gym, accommodation, a maintenance facility and a refuelling tanker. 'I put two aircraft and twenty soldiers there so we could respond at short notice to the General's requirements', said Leakey.

The main body of the squadron remained at Petrovec, where it had the use of hard standing and Macedonian air force hangars to allow full engine changes and the replacement of gear boxes. Petrovec was also the logistic base for the British forces and many VIPs arrived at its airport for onward movement to Pristina by 659 Squadron.

'We rotated the crews and people back and forth to give everyone a break from the basic conditions at Film City,' said Leakey.

Throughout the summer, NATO helicopters and aircraft were regularly taking off from Petrovec and heading into Kosovo and neighbouring

Gazelle AH.1s of 654 Squadrons took up residence at Pristina airport in May 2000 to provide manned aerial surveillance support to KFOR. (Tim Ripley)

Albania requiring close co-operation with the airport civilian air traffic control authorities. Leakey recalled:

> Macedonia ATC were great once they got used to us and we fitted in smoothly at Petrovec. Tirana ATC were fine as well. We got very well known as we flew around the southern Balkans with the General.
>
> We got to go and see all of Kosovo. We saw the destruction and de-populated villages, as well as evidence of the NATO bombing campaign. The destruction is horrendous. We set up a project to get a school at Kliena ready for new term to open on 1st September. I had the squadron down cleaning out rooms and then handed out ten boxes of toys collected in the UK and Germany.

At the end of August, 659 Squadron packed up and returned to Wattisham, its seven-month tour of duty complete. 653 Squadron briefly replaced it for six weeks until ARRC Headquarters left Kosovo.

Leakey said it was a big learning curve being the first helicopter unit in a new theatre. He highlighted that the uncertainty was a constant feature, particularly in terms of logistics, of the squadron's tour because no one was sure how long the squadron would be at Petrovec. Learning to live with a constantly changing threat was another lesson, he said. 'Being flexible and able to respond to the unexpected was very important.'

The Lynx AH.9 performed superbly during the tour, with the squadron's Royal Electrical Mechanical Engineer fitter section having only to change five engines and two gear boxes.

'It was a privilege to command the squadron on an operation such as this,' said Leakey. 'The boys probably don't know how well they did.'

The departure of the Lynx AH.9s in 1999 was not an end to AAC involvement in the British mission to Kosovo. In May 2000 two Westland Gazelle AH.1 helicopters of 654 Squadron AAC deployed to Kosovo to support NATO peacekeeping efforts with their Nitesun airborne searchlight. They join the two RAF Pumas from 33 Squadron, which had been serving in the UN-administered province since June 1999 in a casualty evacuation role. The two contingents had initially worked from separate locations spread around the sprawling Pristina Airport complex and in the autumn of 2000 moved into a new purpose built joint facility on the site. A £1.5 million ($2.13 million) helicopter landing pad and hangar complex was the centre piece of the base, which featured a joint operations room, joint flight planning and joint engineering facilities.

The Gazelles deployed to Kosovo because an manned airborne surveillance capability gap emerged after the Canadian contingents Bell CH-146 Griffon

Gazelle helicopters continued to serve in Kosovo and later in Macedonia during 2000 and 2001. (NATO)

helicopters were withdrawn. After a busy summer in Kosovo, 654 Squadron returned to Wattisham in November to be relieved in November 2000 by the Fleet Air Arm's 847 Naval Air Squadron. The following summer 654 Squadron was back in Kosovo and saw itself drawn into supporting international peacekeeping efforts in neighbouring Macedonia, flying senior officers of NATO's Task Force Harvest around the country on mediation missions.

British involvement in Kosovo would be over by the end of the following year with the last army brigade being withdrawn from the province to allow the British Army to begin preparing for the invasion of Iraq in the spring of 2003.

The AAC continued to provide command detachments of Lynx helicopter to support the NATO and subsequent European Union peacekeeping mission in Bosnia, when the British Army provided senior officers in command positions. 1 Regiment AAC sent a detachment of Lynx to support Major General Richard Dannatt when he led NATO's Stabilization Force in Sarajevo in 2001. The regiment later provided a year-long detachment in Banja Luka when the British Army led the NATO force in north-west Bosnia in 2006–7; this was after 3 Regiment and 4 Regiment provided detachments during 2004 and 2005.

The AAC's involvement in the Balkans ended in 2007 after more than a decade of almost continuous operations in the unstable region.

Chapter 6

3 Regiment AAC Aviation
Battlegroup in Iraq, 2003

For a month in the spring of 2003, the army aviators of 3 Regiment Army Air Corps (AAC) duelled with Iraqi tank and artillery gunners trying to hold back British and US troops from occupying their country. Although the battle subsequently appeared to be hopelessly one-sided, as the men and women of 3 Regiment took to the skies over southern Iraq in March and April 2003, their enemies were far from beaten.

Operation Telic, as the British participation in the US-led invasion of Iraq was code-named, saw the first and only time that an AAC aviation battlegroup has been committed to high intensity combat operations. The four-week long combat phase of the war, saw 3 Regiment's Westland Lynx AH.7s and Gazelle AH.1s at first flying daily aviation reconnaissance patrols (ARPs) to find and engage Iraqi tanks in the deserts and decaying industrial landscape to the west of the southern Iraqi city of Basra. Subsequently, a large contingent of 3 Regiment's helicopters was drafted to support 7 Armoured Brigade's push to drive the Iraqi defenders out of the city of Basra.

For the AAC the commitment of 3 Regiment to Operation Telic, as part of 16 Air Assault Brigade, was the culmination of a decade's work to reconfigure its combat forces for post-Cold War missions. Unlike in the days of the East-West confrontation in Germany when the AAC had a defensive role to engage advancing Soviet tank columns, this time 3 Regiment would be spearheading 16 Brigade's offensive into Iraq. The first AgustaWestland Apache AH.1 attack helicopters in the process of being delivered to the AAC and the Iraq war were seen as a dress rehearsal for the use of army aviation in aggressive air manoeuvre operations.

The preparations for deploying 3 Regiment to the Middle East were far from happy and many of its pilots and ground personnel were amazed that the unit actually got to Iraq in a fit state to go to war.

As the Joint Helicopter Command's Lead Aviation Task Force, 3 Regiment was the UK-designated Army very high readiness helicopter unit when war planning accelerated in the autumn of 2002 it came as no surprise that it was alerted for possible deployment. The UK's initial commitment was to provide an amphibious brigade, of some 3,000 to 5,000 troops backed by a naval task group, to help the US Marines secure Iraq's oil infrastructure on the Al Faw peninsula at the southern tip of Iraq. This then grew to offering a division of troops to help a US offensive from Turkey into northern Iraq. At this point 3 Regiment AAC, was warned off so that it could be sent to join the British division deploying Turkey. The paranoid security clampdown ordered to prevent leaks to the media about British war-planning meant that only a few senior officers in the regiment were told about their potential involvement. The 16 Brigade staff had no idea that one of their major units had been assigned a war role. Although the brigade was told of its possible involvement just before Christmas 2002, the Turkey option was not yet confirmed because the Ankara government had decided to let its parliament vote on its participation in the coming war with Iraq.

The advance of British troops into Iraq in March 2003 was spearheaded by the aviation battlegroup of 3 Regiment AAC. (AgustaWestland)

At Wattisham, 3 Regiment was in overdrive trying to get ready to go to war. A pool of helicopters was fitted with the latest secure radios, sand filters for the engine intakes and radar warning receivers had to be gathered from across the AAC's fleet. These were drawn from the pool of aircraft that had been similarly modified for the 1991 Gulf War and the Kurdish refugee protection mission and so they became known as Op Hamden aircraft, after the code name of that later operation. Then just at the point when it looked like the regiment had enough helicopters of the required standard, it was ordered to hand over four of its best equipped Op Hamden Lynx AH.7s to 847 Naval Air Squadron, which were part of 3 Commando Brigade and had been moved up the deployment schedule. This scarcity of aircraft meant that many air and ground crew only got to train on fully equipped helicopters when they got to the Middle East. As 3 Regiment was in the process of pre-paring to convert to the Apache its manpower had been reduced, requiring a last-minute trawl for scores of personnel from 1, 4 and 9 Regiments AAC to fill out many key positions.

Forward arming and refuelling points in the Iraqi desert supported 3 Regiment operations. (AgustaWestland)

A month passed until the British government decided that the Turkey option was a no go. The UK would now deploy an armoured division of 28,000 troops to Kuwait to support the southern axis of the advance into Iraq. The capture of the oil infrastructure on the Al Faw peninsula by 3 Commando Brigade was to be the UK's main effort and this operation was to begin at the start of the US-led assault on Iraq. The I Marine Expeditionary Force (I MEF) would then storm across the border from Kuwait to capture the Rumaylah oilfield complex and then turn east to screen Basra, to allow the US Army's V Corps to start its drive on Baghdad. In the wake of I MEF, 7 Armoured Brigade, known as the Desert Rats, was then to take over the job of screening Basra and prepare to take on the Iraqi 6th Armoured Division, which was based to the north-west of the city up the Euphrates valley. 16 Brigade was tasked with taking over security of the Rumaylah oilfield, which contained most of Iraq's oil reserves, from the US Marines. This area was criss-crossed with oil pipelines that could not be crossed by the heavy armoured vehicles of 7 Brigade without causing huge damage to the oil pipelines.

A key role in this operation was assigned to 3 Regiment, which took two sub-units, 662 and 663 Squadrons, with it to the Middle East, equipped with ten Lynx AH.7s, two Lynx AH.9s and ten Gazelle AH.1 helicopters.

British brigade deployments in southern Iraq, March–April 2003.

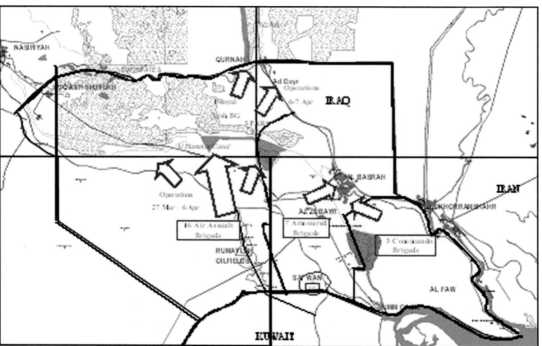

3 Regiment was designated as an aviation battlegroup for the upcoming operation. It contained a mix of Lynx AH.7s armed with TOW wired-guided missiles, two Lynx AH.9 liaison helicopters, which were used as airborne command posts, and Gazelle AH.1 scout helicopters. It was usual to have a company of Paratroopers or Royal Irish Regiment air assault infantry attached to 3 Regiment to provide protection of its forward arming and refuelling points (FARPs) or to hold ground.

Once 16 Brigade got the word to deploy on 20 January 2003, pandemonium ensued at its bases in Colchester, Wattisham and Canterbury. The delays in authorizing the brigade's deployment and the short time frame before deployment meant all this preparatory activity had to be done in a few days to allow the 1,800 vehicles, cargo containers and twenty-two helicopters to be loaded onto several cargo ships for the three week-long voyage to Kuwait. All of 3 Regiment's helicopter, vehicles heavy equipment had to be moved to Kuwait on five ships because there was no spare air transport capacity.

When the ships carrying 3 Regiment's equipment arrived in Kuwait the docks were full with US and British ships unloading cargo. It took weeks to sort out whom each container belonged to and this process was not complete by the time the war started on 19 March. The regiment's helicopters were rebuilt on the dockside in Kuwait's main port and then flown out into the main base of 16 Brigade, in the desert a few miles from the Iraqi border.

After President Bush declared on 18 March that the Iraqis had not met his demands to disarm, all coalition forces in Kuwait were placed in a heightened alert. US commanders expected to launch their offensive by Friday 21 March but events in Baghdad conspired to force this to be brought forward by two days.

At 3 a.m. on 20 March, US Army and Marine Corps columns started bull-dozing lanes through the sand ramp or berm along the Iraq-Kuwait border to open routes northwards. By dawn, thousands of US armoured vehicles were heading towards Basra and Baghdad. Simultaneously with the land assault, 3 Commando Brigade had landed on Al Faw to capture Iraq's oil installations.

In the Kuwaiti desert, 16 Brigade had moved out of its tented camps during the night of 19/20 March to a number of tactical assembly areas to reduce their vulnerability to Iraqi ballistic missile and rocket attacks. The Iraqis fired a number of ballistic missiles at the Kuwait desert prompting coalition troops to don their full chemical warfare protective equipment on several occasions. For a day, the British Army waited in their assembly areas for the Americans to secure their objectives in southern Iraq. During the evening, orders were issued for 16 Brigade to move forward and Royal Engineers of 51 Field Squadron began bulldozing a breach in the Iraqi berm in the early hours of 21 March. Its infantry regiments then began to enter Iraq

British commanders monitored air operations in real time using an 'air picture' downloaded into their headquarters from US and British E-3 AWACSs radar aircraft. (Private Collection)

on the back of trucks. Helicopter crews had flown their Lynx and Gazelles to tactical assembly area, just south of the Iraqi border, to be ready to fly deep into Iraq.

As this was happening, 3 Regiment began preparing to dispatch aviation reconnaissance patrols (ARPs) northwards to the Rumalyah bridge over the al-Hammar canal to try to give warning of a counter-attack by the Iraqi 6th Armoured Division, which was based to the north of the canal. The first reconnaissance missions were flown by 662 Squadron on the morning of 22 March and at first there was little sign of enemy activity. These patrols involved a pair of helicopters, a Lynx and a Gazelle, which worked as a team. The unarmed Gazelles acted as the eyes and ears for the TOW-armed Lynx. This was necessary because the TOW missile required the Lynx to hover or fly in a straight line as it fired its weapons, making it very vulnerable to enemy fire. By using the Gazelle to scout for targets, the ARP concept was meant to minimize the time the Lynx had to show itself to engage targets.

Truck convoys of 3 Regiment's supply echelon had now moved into Iraq to set up a FARP to enhance the ability of the regiment to support 16 Brigade's rapidly advancing troops. Although the oilfield infrastructure was secured intact, the whole of the 16 Brigade area was littered with the remnants of an Iraqi mechanized brigade that had been rolled over by the US Marines. Paratroopers and Royal Irish patrols fanned out to round up the prisoners, make contact with the local population and set up a security perimeter to stop any Iraqi counter-attacks. The size of the security zone was so big that helicopter patrols by 3 Regiment were the only way to monitor it all and give any kind of early warning of any Iraqi forces massing nearby. The Lynx of 662 Squadron started to fly small groups of Royal Irish Regiment soldiers to set up snap or 'Eagle' vehicle checkpoints to monitor civilian traffic on the main roads.

Iraqi tanks were the main target of 3 Regiment's TOW-armed Lynx AH.7s during Operation Telic. (Tim Ripley)

While 16 Brigade was mopping up in the Rumalyah oilfields, 7 Armoured Brigade was moving north towards the outskirts of Basra and the US Marines were approaching Nasiriyah. Iraqi forces in both of these cities were now starting to put up serious resistance. By the evening on 23 March, senior British and American commanders were beginning to realize that the Iraqi collapse was not going to happen in the next couple of days and more resources were needed to deal with Basra and Nasiriyah.

Major General Robin Brims, the commander of the British division, was not yet ready to assault the city but he wanted to stage a series of operations to specifically target centres of resistance. He did not want to fight a prolonged street battle with the Iraqis that could cause heavy civilian casualties. A series of very violent skirmishes between Iraqi and British troops now broke out on the outer fringes of Basra. To help in these engagements, General Brims called forward two Gazelles and three Lynx from 662 Squadron on 25 March. They set up a forward operating base at the disused Shaibah airfield to the south-west of Basra. In the early hours of the following morning, the Lynx staged a raid on Iraqi troops occupying a factory complex, destroying four buildings, an ammo dump and a water tower with TOW missiles. The 662 Squadron detachment remained at Shaibah for several more days and was increasingly drawn into the battle for Basra. On 28 March, two of its Lynx discovered and destroyed two heavily armed Iraqi militia 'technical' vehicles with two TOW missiles. This was a major achievement because 3 Regiment was starting to find that the TOW missile had several limitations, including a tendency to 'hang-up' when the missile's rocket motors failed to fire and dropped down below the helicopter spooling out the guidance wire. Unless these wires were immediately cut, they could become entangled in the helicopters tail rotors.

Back in 16 Brigade's area, 663 Squadron had to spend the night re-building its FARP after a huge dust storm swept through it. 16 Brigade was now ordered to focus on containing the Iraqi 6th Armoured Division north of the al-Hammer canal. ARPs of 3 Regiment were ordered to probe along the canal to find the centre of Iraqi resistance and called down artillery fire and air strikes. At dawn on 28 March, a Lynx and Gazelle from 663 Squadron made the first ever ARP over the forward line of British troops into enemy territory.

For over a week, this battle grew in intensity as 16 Brigade pushed its reconnaissance forces further north from the al-Hammer canal towards the Euphrates River and the main defensive positions of the Iraqi division. The terrain between the al-Hammer canal and the Euphrates River alternated between palm groves and marshy ground, so there was plenty of opportunity for the Iraqis to hide their positions.

Royal Artillery 105mm artillery batteries co-ordinated their fire missions with Lynx-armed helicopter missions to ensure Iraqi troops were kept under around-the-clock pressure. (BAE Systems)

3 Regiment's Lynx joined the battle engaging targets with TOW missiles or calling in artillery fire. Iraqi armour was engaged for the first time by 663 Squadron at 8.25 a.m. on 28 March. An hour later, the squadron engaged more Iraqi tanks with a barrage of twelve TOW missiles, destroying two T-55s. Later in the day, the squadron also destroyed a BMP armoured personnel carrier.

This was by no means a one-sided battle, with the Iraqis making extensive use of their own target location systems to control their return artillery fire. British Lynx pilots on an hourly basis had to dodge Iraqi tank, artillery and mortar fire that was aimed at their helicopters and if they got too close to Iraqi infantry, volleys of rocket-propelled grenades could be expected. In effect, 3 Regiment was playing a deadly game of cat and mouse with several thousand Iraqi defenders, who had by no means given up the fight. The 6th Division conducted a professional defensive operation and gave as good as it got on many occasions.

In one typical incident during this period, Iraqi artillery and tank shells were exploding amid the Scimitar armoured vehicles of the Household

Southern Iraq as seen from a British helicopter in 2003. (Tim Ripley)

Cavalry Regiment (HCR). An ARP of Lynx and Gazelle helicopters from 3 Regiment led by Captain Richard Cuthill arrived overhead to give fire support. With visibility obscured by sand thrown up by the Iraqi fire, Cuthill manoeuvred his Lynx to behind the Scimitars so he could line up his helicopters to fire along the path of 30mm tracer rounds fired by the HCR vehicles. He spotted the muzzle flash of an Iraqi self-propelled artillery piece and guided a TOW missile onto its targets. This required him to fly his helicopter straight and level as shells exploded around it. This bravery won Cuthill the Distinguished Flying Cross.

In the first week of April, British troops were closing in on Basra and the Brigade released 3 PARA to join this operation and it moved eastwards to be ready to help in what could be a huge street battle. Simultaneously, 16 Brigade was ordered to make preparations to assault the 6th Division's positions at Ad Dayr and Al Qurnah to seize key bridges over the Euphrates. Reconnaissance teams had closed up to these positions and were engaged

RAF Puma HC.1 support helicopters joined 3 Regiment to monitor a huge area of southern Iraq as the bulk of the British force concentrated on the drive into Basra. (Private collection)

Gazelle AH.1 helicopters teamed up with Lynx AH.7s to form armed reconnaissance patrols to engage Iraqi armour. (Op Telic Media Pool)

in skirmishing with well-camouflaged apparently determined Iraqi troops. 3 Regiment also began to send out ARPs far to the west towards Nasiriyah to protect the main supply route to the big US Army logistic base on the outskirts of the town. The aviation battlegroup was also given the job of securing the Rumalyah gas and oil complex, with ARPs, an attached RAF Westland Puma HC.1 transport helicopter and ground patrols from attached infantry units. Its helicopters and attached units were responsible for the security of some 6,000 square kilometres of southern Iraq.

Resistance in Basra appeared to be faltering and this was the cue for 3 Regiment to ramp up its support for 7 Brigade, with a regular rotation of ARPs now organized to overfly the outskirts of Basra. One 662 Squadron ARP was engaged by an Iraqi surface-to-air missile on 3 April, indicating that there was still some fight left in Iraqi defenders of Basra.

On 6 April, as US troops entered Baghdad, the leader of Iraqi resistance in Basra, Ali Hassan al-Majid – the infamous Chemical Ali – reportedly fled north from the city with several of his key lieutenants. This was the moment General Brims had been waiting for and he ordered 7 Brigade to sweep into the city. The old kasbah district of the city was 3rd Battalion, The Parachute Regiment's objective and the Paratroopers moved forward expecting to meet heavy resistance. 662 Squadron flew a show of force over the city as the Desert Rats and Paras, were ready to undertake precision strikes on centres of resistance. The advance on the morning on 7 April proved an anti-climax with cheering crowds of locals filling the streets to welcome the British troops. The Fedayeen were long gone. As British troops fanned out through the city later in the day and on 8 April, 662 Squadron remained in the air overhead but its firepower was not required.

Further to the north-west, 16 Brigade was scheduled to launch its own strike on 7 April to neutralize the 6th Division and launch a drive towards Al Amara but the Iraqi defenders had fled. Thus began 16 Brigade's drive northwards. Convoys of The Parachute Regiment and Royal Irish vehicles raced forward to capture intact the bridges over the Euphrates, with helicopters of 3 Regiment flying top cover. Huge crowds of civilians lined the roads as the British troops surged forwards into Maysan province. The Iraqi army had now collapsed.

British troops were assigned responsibility for securing the south-east of Iraq and they were ordered to move quickly to establish control of all major towns in the region. On 12 April, the Royal Irish Regiment moved

Lynx AH.7s were the mainstay of the AAC campaign in southern Iraq in 2003. (AgustaWestland)

into Al Amara and 16 Brigade's Headquarters followed a few days later. 3 Regiment handed over control of the Rumalyah oilfield and flew north to set up a new forward operating base at Al Amara airfield on the western outskirts of the town to allow it to support 16 Brigade's attempts to rebuild Maysan province.

During the days after the Iraqi collapse, 3 Regiment suffered its only loss when a Gazelle of 662 Squadron was severely damaged after it struck a power cable on 11 April. This followed a similar incident three days earlier to a Gazelle of 662 Squadron, but that helicopter managed to safely return to its base.

This was a very chaotic situation with rival militia and insurgent groups all vying for power in the province. Looting was rampant and no police were to be seen. British soldiers took on trying to get public utilities working, clamping down on lawlessness and trying to tidy up the detritus of war.

3 Regiment remained in Maysan through to the end of May and then began to pack up its helicopters and equipment to return home. 7 Brigade took over control of Maysan province on 29 May. To support the re-configured British occupation force, 662 Squadron remained behind with four Gazelles and four Lynx, based at Basra International Airport, which was now the centre of all British aviation operations in Iraq. The squadron remained in place for another month until troops of 4 Regiment AAC began arriving from Wattisham for a six-month tour of duty.

This brought 3 Regiment's war to an end. The regiment had played a key part in 16 Brigade's blitzkrieg advance through Iraq giving crucial air support to 7 Brigade's drive on Basra. At the end of the war, 16 Brigade claimed the destruction of 86 Iraqi tank, as well as hundreds of other vehicles and weapons. Out of these 3 Regiment claimed four T-55s, two 2S1 self-propelled artillery pieces, a D30 howitzer, a BMP armoured vehicle and two 'technical' vehicles. Working as an aviation battlegroup, 3 Regiment had shown the utility of assigning helicopters to work for specific army brigades rather than massing them under a central command. However, the situation in post-Saddam Iraq was very different. For the next five years the AAC would have to fight a very different type of war.

Chapter 7

Phoenix During the Invasion of Iraq, 2003

From on board a Royal Navy Westland Sea King AEW.9 helicopter flying high over southern Iraq in March 2003, the Iraqi armour column was clearly visible on the radar screen in rear cabin. The battalion, led by T-55 tanks, MLTB armoured personnel carriers and ZSU-23-4 self-propelled anti-aircraft guns, had gathered on the southern edge of Basra city and was now heading towards British lines. A brief radio message from the Sea King's crew alerted the Royal Artillery command centre, at the 1 (UK) Armoured Division headquarters in northern Kuwait, and within minutes a Phoenix UAV was diverted from its patrol area to look for Iraqi armour. When the Phoenix arrived overhead an imagery analysts, in the ground control station, took a quick look at the first video imagery and immediately identified them as a hostile force. The team of operators controlling the UAV, then began directed Royal Artillery AS-90 155mm self-propelled gunfire on to the column. When the first shells landed, the plumes of smoke could be clearly seen on the video imagery and allowed the operators to successfully adjust the fire to bring the rain of shells on targets.

The job was far from done and the Phoenix operators began calling in the first of thirty-six air strikes by coalition strike jets against the Iraqi armour before a US Marine Corps Bell AH-1W Cobra arrived to continue directing the airpower into action. Within three hours the desert outside Basra was littered with the burning hulks of sixty vehicles. Those who had doubted that the British Army could use UAVs successfully in battle had been proved wrong.

When the British government ordered more than 40,000 troops to Kuwait in January 2003 as part of the build-up for the invasion of Iraq, it was not surprising that a contingent of Phoenix UAVs would be part of the force package.

Two UAV batteries and a regimental headquarters battery had recently been brought together to create the British Army's first specialist UAV unit, designated 32nd Regiment Royal Artillery. This would be the first time the British Army had deployed a regimental sized UAV unit in a real combat operation. The regiment had participated in Exercise Saif Sareea II in Oman in the autumn of 2001 and a number of exercises to try to build up the expertise and procedures needed to integrate UAVs into a large formation of troops.

However, for Royal Artillery UAV operators, as well as the commanders and units they were supporting, this was a new experience and there was a feeling they would be 'learning on the job' how to use the Phoenix to maximum effect in a high-intensity combat operation.

Like the rest of 1 (UK) Armoured Division, 32nd Regiment spent the last month of 2002 and the first couple of months of 2003 in some turmoil as first the unit was alerted to deploy to Turkey as part of the northern front of the coming war against Iraq. By January, this option was scrapped after the Turkey's refused to allow US and British troops to invade Iraq from their territory, so the British Army was switched to deploying to Kuwait to join the US southern push. At the same time, 32nd Regiment had to contribute

Phoenix unmanned aerial vehicles played a key role in the British invasion of southern Iraq in March and April 2003. (Private collection)

British artillery shells strike an Iraqi armoured column, as seen through the thermal imaging cameras of a Phoenix unmanned aerial vehicle. (BAE Systems)

personnel to help with fire-fighting duty after the British government ordered armed forces to provide emergency cover during a firemen's strike.

The eventual intelligence, surveillance, targeting acquisition and reconnaissance (ISTAR) force package comprised 18 (newly converted to Phoenix from Multiple Launch Rocket System) and 22 Batteries, as well as the Regimental Tactical Party (Tac Party), the regimental Echelon to provide logistic support and K Battery, equipped with the Ericsson Mamba counter-battery radar, from 5th Regiment Royal Artillery. Acoustic Locating and signals intelligence units to listen to Iraqi radio traffic were also attached to the 1 (UK) Division's ISTAR Group. 32nd Regiment took nearly 400 troops to Kuwait, as well as more than 100 vehicles and hundreds of large ISO containers containing spares and the other specialist equipment needed to keep its Phoenix flying for an indeterminate period. Some eighty-nine Phoenix air vehicles – more than half the number left in the army's inventory – were sent indicating the importance placed on the deployment.

The ships carrying 32nd Regiment's equipment started arriving in Kuwait in February and personnel who had arrived by chartered airliners began collecting their vehicles and driving out into a series of temporary tented camps in the northern Kuwaiti desert, close to the Iraq border. Then work

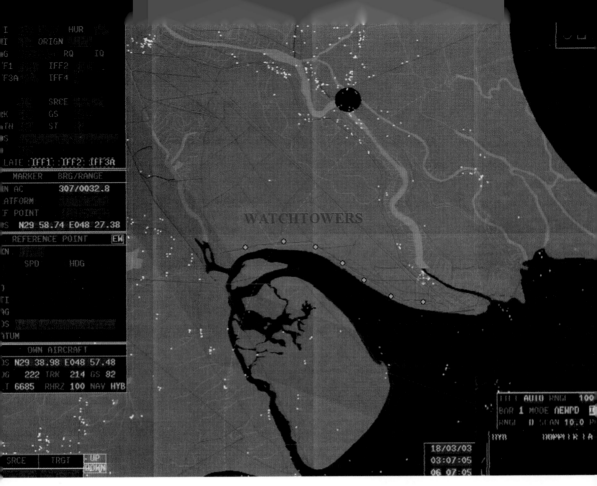

I   HUR
I   ORIGN
G   RQ   IQ
F1   IFF2
F3A   IFF4

SRCE
K   GS
TH   ST
S

LATE IFF1 IFF2 IFF3A
MARKER   BRG/RANGE
N AC   307/0032.8
ATFORM
F POINT
S N29 58.74 E048 27.38
REFERENCE POINT EW
N
SPD   HDG

I
G
S
TUM

OWN AIRCRAFT
S N29 38.98 E048 57.48
G 222 TRK 214 GS 82
T 6685 RHRZ 100 NAV HYB

WATCHTOWERS

AUTO RNG 100
BAR 1 MODE NEWPD
RNG 0 SCAN 10.0

18/03/03
03:07:05
06 07:05

SRCE   TRGT UP

Iraq tank movements were monitored in real-time Sea King ASAC.7 radar helicopters and Phoenix unmanned aerial vehicles were tasked to investigate radar contacts. (Thales)

began to make the regiment ready to support on-going operations, including establishing launch sites and establishing communications with the 1 (UK) Division's headquarters. This proved the crucial part of 32nd Regiment's preparations for war and saw the Regimental Tac Party fully integrated into the divisional artillery command and control organization, under the command of a Royal Artillery brigadier.

The Tac Party took a ground station with it that allowed Phoenix imagery to be viewed in the divisional headquarters and the fibre optic link developed for use in Kosovo was re-used to allow several staff branches in the headquarters to watch the imagery in real time or record it. However, the analogue nature of the Phoenix imagery meant it could not he transmitted across satellite communications to be viewed in other British headquarters in the Middle East or back in the UK.

Although the Phoenix had not been used in major combat operations before, the commander of 1 (UK) Division, Major General Robin Brims, and his senior staff were keen to use it as much as possible. Along with the

Mamba radar, Acoustic Locating and signals intelligence assets, the Phoenix were under the direct control of the divisional headquarters and they could task it as General Brims wished. Other ISTAR systems such as RAF Panavia Tornado GR4 and BAE Systems Harrier GR7s fitted with reconnaissance pods and USAF General Atomics MQ-1 Predators were controlled by other headquarters and were only allocated to support British operations in southern Iraq on high priority missions. These were very rare because the US push on Baghdad was the strategic main effort of the coalition and it received priority for coalition ISTAR support.

The flat desert terrain of southern Iraq, however, proved ideal for Phoenix operations, allowing the air vehicles to operate far from their ground control stations uninhibited by hills that might have interrupted the system's line of sight data links. This usual 50-kilometre radius of action of the Phoenix from its launch station could be pushed to the limit over southern Iraq with 80 to 100 kilometres now being the norm and on one occasion a mission was flown 120 kilometres from a ground data terminal.

The first launching sites were established in northern Kuwait ready to support the initial move over the border into southern Iraq. As British Royal

British Warrior armoured infantry battalions were in the forefront of the campaign to surround the southern city of Basra. (BAE Systems)

Imagery analysts in the Phoenix ground control stations then identified targets for air or artillery attack. (BAE Systems)

Marines landed on the Al Faw peninsula and columns of Challenger tanks from 7 Armoured Brigade crossed the border, Phoenix UAVs were operating above them looking for hostile threats and Iraqi troop movements.

The two Phoenix batteries contained their own Tac Parties, which were dispatched as the tactical situation demanded to work with British infantry and armoured battlegroups operating in southern Iraq. These Tac Parties did not have down links to see Phoenix imagery direct but had direct radio links to the ground control stations to talk to operators and imagery analysts as missions unfolded so they could pass on relevant information to the infantry and tanks commanders they were working with. The crews in the ground control stations were qualified artillery observers who counted, called for and directed artillery fire if suitable targets were fired. The Tac Parties also played a key role in educating infantry and tank commanders, many of whom had never worked with UAVs before, on what Phoenix could do for them.

The real challenge for General Brims and his senior commanders was working out where to position Phoenix air vehicles so they could provide useful information. Here the Mamba radars and signals intelligence units proved crucial in detecting the position of Iraq artillery and mortar batteries firing on British troops. Once fire was detected, the Mamba teams would pass the co-ordinates of Iraq gun batteries to the Phoenix operators so they could task an air vehicle to take a look. The use of 'shoot and scoot' tactics by the Iraqis meant that Phoenix was a key way of tracking Iraqi gun batteries as they tried to move to safety after firing at the British.

A bigger problem was detecting any massing of Iraqi troops and tanks as they prepared counter-attacks. The only wide area ISTAR asset in the British force was the Westland Sea King Mk 7 airborne early warning helicopters embarked on the aircraft carrier HMS *Ark Royal* cruising in the northern Arabian Gulf. The Sea Kings were fitted with Thales Searchwater 2000 radars, which could operate in a ground moving target indicator (GMTI) mode that could pick up columns of tanks or trucks moving around the desert.

In early 2003, the British Army did not have any kind of battlefield internet-type network communications system so both the Mamba and Sea King crews had to report suspicious contacts to 32nd Regiment's command team by 'steam drive' voice radio messages. This relied on the speed and accuracy of the Royal Artillery radio operators and staff officers to take down the details and then pass them to Phoenix operators for action. Once targets were detected, voice radio messages were also the primary means to task ground troops, artillery or aircraft to attack them.

Phoenix launch detachments moved forwards behind the first wave of British armour to ensure maximum surveillance coverage of southern Iraq. (Private collection)

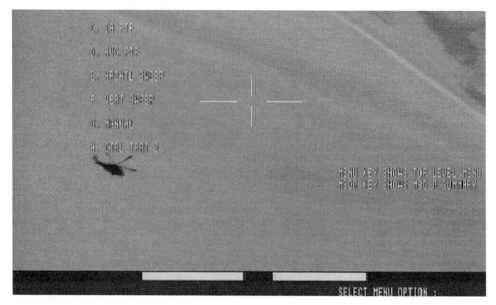

The shadow of a helicopter as seen through a Phoenix night vision camera illustrates the need to properly deconflict helicopters from unmanned aerial vehicles. (BAE Systems)

Royal Artillery personnel in Phoenix ground control stations were fully qualified to call in artillery strikes on valid Iraqi targets. (BAE Systems)

The main body British division was not in the first wave of the invasion force as it crossed in Iraq during the early hours of 20 March 2003. Units of the US Marine Corps I Marine Expeditionary Force (I MEF) had the initial tasks of destroying and then pushing through the Iraqi border defences to the south of Basra. The plan then called for 1 (UK) Division to relieve the I MEF in place to allow it to join the main push on Basra. General Brims' troops would have the job of screening and eventually capturing Basra to protect the rear supply lines of the main US attack force. The first Phoenix mission of Operation Telic, as the British mission to Iraq was now code-named, was flown at 19.26 hours local time on 19 March by 18 Battery, making it the first UK force element to cross the international border into Iraq.

The one exception to this was 3 Commando Brigade, which was tasked to land troops in on the Al Faw peninsula to secure Iraqi oil installations to prevent the Iraqi regime releasing oil into the northern Arabian Sea in an act of 'ecological terrorism'. The majority of Phoenix missions flown in the first couple of days of the operation were conducted in support of the Royal Marines as they fought to drive Iraq troops up the peninsula and back towards Basra.

During 21 March, I MEF began handing over responsibility for the desert outside Basra to British forces and battlegroups of 7 Armoured Brigade

AS-90 self-propelled guns rained 155mm artillery shells on Iraqi targets identified by Phoenix UAVs. (BAE Systems)

started to move forward and begin to engage isolated detachment of Iraqi troops on the southern suburbs of the city. US troops had now become engaged in bitter fighting with Iraqi troops in the city of Nasiriyah, 150 kilometres to the north-west. General Brims and his brigade commanders decided to halt the British advance outside of Basra to avoid a bloody battle that would cause unnecessary military and civilian casualties. The aim was to screen the city with troops and launch 'raids' against centres of resistance until the grip of Saddam Hussein's regime was so weakened that British troops could push into Basra unopposed.

Now was the time for Phoenix come into its own as a surveillance tool giving British commanders and unprecedented view of what was happening inside the teeming city that was base to thousands pro-Saddam Hussein guerrilla fighters.

Royal Artillery repair teams worked around the clock to repair damaged Phoenix to get them back in to service. (Private collection)

Sea King ASAC.7s flew daily missions from HMS *Ark Royal* in northern Arabian Gulf to pinpoint targets for further investigation by Phoenix unmanned aerial vehicles. (Tim Ripley)

Anti-regime demonstrations and other activity in the city was watched in real time by British commanders, who were trying to judge the right moment to deliver the *coup de grâce* against Iraqi forces in Basra. The Iraqis were not unaware of the role played by the Phoenix and on several occasions they successfully engaged the British UAVs with anti-aircraft fire, bringing down at least half a dozen air vehicles.

32nd Regiment now began to move into its battle rhythm, launching air vehicles around the clock for the next three weeks to support British troops around Basra.

Daily planning meetings in 1 (UK) Division headquarters allocated air vehicles and ground control stations to meet the requirements of General Brims' battle plan. Areas of interest were allocated for Phoenix to watch for extended periods of time. This often required launch vehicles and ground

107

control stations to move forwards close to the front line to provide the necessary coverage and endurance over the required areas of interest. According to a senior officer of 32nd Regiment, using Phoenix to direct offensive strike with artillery and close air support (CAS) became routine activities.

Dynamic re-tasking of Phoenix was a daily occurrence, particularly when Iraqi forays out of Basra were detected by the Sea King AEW.7s radar.

Co-operation with the Mamba radars of K Battery also soon became a well-oiled procedure and a senior 32nd Regiment officer said once Iraqi mortar fire was detected Phoenix could be re-tasked to identify and confirm their location, before directing AS-90 fire to destroy the target. The 32nd Regiment officer said this type of engagement was routinely completed within seven minutes of the Iraqi mortar opening fire and being detected.

Iraqi battlefield surface-to-surface missile (SSM) batteries operating in the area to the north of Basra were becoming a major irritant for the coalition because they were firing missiles into Kuwait on an almost daily basis. USAF Predator UAVs and British Phoenix were regularly tasked to patrol suspected

The destruction of the Ba'ath Party headquarters in Basra after Phoenix detected hard-line militia fighters entering the building was a major coup for 32nd Regiment Royal Artillery. (Private collection)

Basra's Ba'ath Party headquarters as seen through the night vision camera of a Phoenix unmanned aerial vehicle. (BAE Systems)

missile launch 'boxes'. A senior 32nd Regiment officer described how three Iraqi FROG missile launchers were discovered by a Phoenix and two USAF Fairchild A-10A Warthog attack jets were tasked to take out the missiles.

By the first week of April, the US Army and Marine Corps were on the out-skirts of Baghdad and the Iraqi regime appeared to be teetering on the brink of collapse. Outside Basra, General Brims was making the final preparation for his long-awaited drive into the city.

Phoenix were tasked to maintain observation of Ba'ath Party headquarters in downtown Basra where the notorious Iraqi commander Ali Hassan al-Majid, aka Chemical Ali, was leading the resistance in the city. Some 200 fanatical Fedayeen fighters were detected operating from the building on 5 April and a US Marine Corps McDonnell Douglas F/A-18C Hornet was called up to drop two satellite-guided Joint Direct Attack Munitions (JDAMs) on the target. The building collapsed and scores of the fighters were killed but Chemical Ali had already made his escape, heading north out of the city.

The attack was a graphic demonstration of the waning grip on Basra of the regime. Both the population and the Fedayeen could see the way things were going. General Brims now declared 'conditions were set for regime collapse in Basra' and the following day launched 7 Armoured Brigade into action. As the Desert Rats surged forward under the watchful eye of Phoenix they found the city deserted of the Fedayeen and were greeted by cheering crowds.

This honeymoon period did not last long as the British Army and the population of Basra struggled to get the city functioning again. Rioting mobs ransacked government buildings and utilities such as electricity and water supplies collapsed.

British forces tried to keep order in this chaotic environment and 32nd Regiment found its services were required again. Phoenix missions were flown to support vehicle check points, cordon and search and arrest operations by British troops, as well as observation of activity at border crossing points and choke points and possible smuggling on land and water. Mobile targets were tracked, the perimeters of British bases were patrolled and infrastructure, such as abandoned Iraqi ammunition dumps, electricity pylon lines and oil pipelines were monitored to prevent sabotage. An increasingly important role was monitoring public disorder as the population became more disenchanted with the inability of the British to provide security and the basics of life in the Basra.

As the hot summer heat approached it effectively curtained the participation of Phoenix because of limitations of the air vehicle's flight envelope. By June, 32nd Regiment was packing up its equipment and heading home.

The participation of the Phoenix in the combat and peace support phases of Operation Telic was praised strongly by British commanders and intelligence analysts. On several occasions the real-time imagery provided by Phoenix proved critical in allowing British troops to achieve their objectives.

Numerous British Army commanders said that when Phoenix was allocated to them it greatly increased their situational awareness of what was going on around their units. Post operational tour reports said the Phoenix was responsible for detecting the targets that were on the receiving end of 40 per cent of all UK artillery fire, involving some 22,000 rounds in total. It also directed scores of close air support strikes on Iraqi targets.

Phoenix flew 133 sorties during the war fighting phase and a further 250 in support of the occupation of Basra. Some 23 air vehicles were lost or damaged beyond repair, with only some half a dozen being attributed to Iraqi anti-aircraft fire.

It has long been recognized that the Phoenix was a 'son of the Cold War'. Phoenix was not specifically designed for twenty-first century missions and it had several shortcomings. These included its sheer bulk, which meant its launch vehicle could only be deployed by ship to the operational theatre. The British communications networks both in-theatre and back to the UK just did not have the bandwidth to allow the real-time distribution of Phoenix imagery over large networks.

Even with these limitations, General Brims, the commander of the British invasion force, in several of his official de-brief reports on Operation Telic described Phoenix as one of his four key battle winning equipments, along side the Challenger 2 main battle tank, Warrior infantry fighting vehicle and AS90 self-propelled artillery system.

Chapter 8

Lynx over Iraq – Operation Telic, 2003 to 2009

The Lynx was rocked by the impact of small arms fire on the right side of the aircraft and in the cockpit, all hell broke loose – a large explosion was heard as a 7.62mm round smashed its way through the pilot's door Perspex window, was how Major Scott Watkins, an Australian army aviator attached to 652 Squadron, Army Air Corps, described the first bullet impacts of a insurgent machine gun attack on his Westland Lynx AH.9 helicopter on 10 November 2004. He continues:

> Debris in the form of what can only be described as a fine mist, appeared instantly in front of my pilot, Captain Keith Reesby, in the right seat and then disappeared just as quickly. The smell of cordite pervaded and then there was the yell of pain that immediately followed and the realization that one of the crew had been shot. It is a sound that I will not soon forget.
>
> Despite media reports to the contrary, I was already on the controls at the time of the contact, having decided to do a bit of flying on departure from Camp Dogwood. On hearing the bullet burst into the cockpit, I was able to rapidly roll the aircraft to the left having initially believed the round had come through the floor. As we banked left, I screamed over the VHF radio 'We're hit, we're hit!'
>
> Much to our collective relief, aviation operations in Dogwood had heard the transmission and acknowledged my call. As we continued to turn and track away from the firing point back towards the south, Keith let us know he'd been shot. Dinger, our Air Door Gunner in the back, had already made ready on the GPMG and was preparing to engage the firing point as he observed

it pass through the 6 to 7 o'clock position of the aircraft as it turned. He did advise me that he could now see the shooters but the time had now passed for shooting back and Dinger was instructed to help Keith by passing him field dressings.

While the aircraft was performing as expected and all indications were normal up until this point, we couldn't be sure that she was going to keep flying. The desert represented a relatively safe location to put down should the need suddenly arise. By the grace of God, it didn't. Once over the desert, we turned to track direct for Dogwood. Once on the ground, the aircraft was rolled to a stop with a bit of interesting cross cockpit brake application (the Lynx AH.9 has only one brake lever, which is located on the right side cyclic).

After a rapid shutdown, Keith started to pull himself out of his seat. He was almost all the way out by the time Dinger and I got to him. Despite his wounds, he had remained calm throughout the whole ordeal, never panicking, and communicated with us

Southern Iraq's climate and environment proved to be major challenges for the AAC's helicopter crews. (Basra Media Pool)

regularly as he methodically dressed his own wounds. His calm and collected disposition significantly reduced the burden on the crew as we raced to get him to Dogwood.

Assistance came quickly in the form of our aviation operations personnel and the RAF refuellers. They raced to the front of the aircraft where Keith was now sitting and soon had him in an ambulance and off to the Black Watch Regimental Aid Post. Within fifteen minutes he was in an American Army Blackhawk medevac helicopter and would arrive at a Baghdad hospital less than an hour after the actual shooting.

For his coolness under fire, which undoubtedly saved the life of his pilot, Major Watkins was awarded the Distinguished Flying Cross, Britain's third highest decoration for bravery. Captain Reesby made a full recovery and only two days later another helicopter the Australian was flying was attacked south of Baghdad. Again, he did not panic but followed his attackers as they sped away in a car, leading to their arrest and the discovery of grenades, shells and bomb-making equipment.

For the Lynx crews of the AAC who bore the brunt of providing light utility support to the British garrison in southern Iraq from 2003 to 2009 the

Night missions were a central feature of AAC operations in Iraq because of the hot climate in the summer months. (AgustaWestland)

incident near Camp Dogwood, during the deployment of the Black Watch Battlegroup to support the Battle for Fallujah in November 2004, was a grim reminder of the daily dangers they faced. During Operation Telic, as the British campaign in Iraq was code-named, the AAC suffered two fatalities, of which only one occurred in combat. Captain David Ian Dobson, was serving as an exchange pilot with 847 Naval Air Squadron, when his Lynx was shot down over central Basra by an insurgent anti-aircraft missile in May 2006. Lance Corporal David Kenneth Wilson, of 659 Squadron, was killed in a non-combat incident at Basra airbase in December 2008.

Every AAC Lynx squadron sent personnel to Iraq during the course of the British campaign and the helicopter's participation defined the light-utility role for a generation of British Army aviators. Over the six years of the campaign, the AAC and its sister Fleet Air Arm Lynx unit, 847 Squadron, on two occasions provided continuous light-utility helicopter support to the twelve British Army brigades that deployed for occupation duty in Basra.

Keeping helicopters flying in Iraq's harsh environment required intense maintenance by ground crews. (Basra Media Pool)

Although events on the ground changed dramatically from tour to tour, for the Lynx squadrons Operation Telic had a certain predictability, at least during the preparation and arrival at Basra airbase on the outside of the main city in the south of the country, which was the focus of British operations.

Operation Telic AAC Squadron Deployments, 2003 to 2009

Tour dates	Squadrons	Aircraft type
Jan 03 to June 03	662 & 663 Sqns	Lynx AH.7 & Gazelle AH.1
Jul 03 to Nov 03	654 Sqn	Lynx AH.7 & Gazelle AH.1
Nov 03 to Apr 04	659 Sqn	Lynx AH.7 & Gazelle AH.1
May 04 to Sept 04	669 Sqn	Lynx AH.7
Sept 04 to Mar 05	652 Sqn	Lynx AH.7 & Lynx AH.9
Apr 05 to Dec 05	659 Sqn	Lynx AH.7
Jan 06 to Jun 06	847 Sqn	Lynx AH.7
Jun 06 to Nov 06	664 Sqn	Lynx AH.7
Dec 07 to May 07	659 Sqn	Lynx AH.7
May 07 to Oct 07	652 Sqn	Lynx AH.9
Nov 07 to Feb 08	847 Sqn	Lynx AH.9
Feb 08 to Jun 08	672 Sqn	Lynx AH.9
Jul 08 to Dec 08	651 Sqn	Lynx AH.9
Jan to Jun 09	659 Sqn	Lynx AH.9

Each squadron usually deployed with around eighty personnel, including some twenty-one aircrew, for six months at a time. Each squadron was alerted that it was to deploy with a specific army brigade several months in advance to allow it to participate in the brigade's pre-deployment training. This allowed the aviators to get to know the units and senior commanders to get some insight into the tactics and procedures that would be used during the deployment.

Except in the summer of 2003, when the occupation period began and 4 Regiment relieved 3 Regiment, which had participated in the war fighting phase of the campaign, AAC squadrons did not take their own helicopters with them but took over those already at Basra from the unit they were relieving. These aircraft were part of a small pool of helicopters modified to theatre entry standard (TES) and fitted with the latest defensive systems, armour, weapons, secure communications, dust screens and heat dissipaters for the engines. Known as Operation Telic helicopters these were rotated home after a specific period in Iraq for major overhaul and when servicing was required rather than when squadrons returned home after six-month tours of duty. So-called relief in-place also involved squadrons taking over officer accommodation, maintenance facilities and vehicles from their predecessors. It was usual for squadrons to rotate some of their personnel back to their home bases during six-month tours to ease the pressure and give as many as possible operational experience.

AAC Lynx detachments in Iraq were always attached to a joint helicopter command and control organization, known as the Joint Helicopter Force (Iraq) (JHF(I)), at Basra airbase. This was headed up in rotation by an AAC lieutenant colonel, Royal Air Force wing commander or Royal Navy commander. The AAC colonel, many of his senior staff and JHF(I) administrative personnel were usually from the parent regiment of the Lynx squadron to provide some degree of continuity.

The JHF(I) was responsible for all helicopter tasking in the British divisional area and its commander was the senior battlefield helicopter advisor to the British general in Basra. It also included representatives of allied helicopters units working in the British area. For the Lynx crews it meant they were working as part of a joint helicopter force and each day a single air plan or air tasking order would be generated by the JHF(I) mission planners. They then got briefed in a centre facility and once airborne listened into command JHF(I) command radio facilities for changes to their tasking or tactical updates.

AAC Lynx helicopters were armed with 7.62mm door guns for self defence during missions over southern Iraq. (Private collection)

Iraq's deserts meant brown-out conditions were always a problem for AAC helicopter pilots. (AgustaWestland)

Life for the Lynx detachment followed a routine that revolved the number of daily task lines or missions. It was usual for the Lynx detachment to have two task lines, which meant in a twenty-four-hour period it had to get two pairs of aircraft airborne for up two hours' time on task. This could be surged in a time of crisis but any sustained increase would require additional servicing or spares.

Flying the Lynx over southern Iraq was a demanding experience, particularly in the heat of summer when temperatures could reach more than 50 degree centigrade. At the height of summer the performance of the basic Lynx AH.7 or 9 was degraded to such a degree that they could only lift one passenger at a time in daylight. This meant that between June and September, the Lynx was allocated primarily night tasks unless the missions were considered a priority. Even in the winter months, when daylight operations were routine, the extra weight from the TES equipment had an impact on performance and if extra passengers were carried then aircraft endurance was degraded by a minute for every extra six kilograms of weight carried.

Lynx pilots recalled that performance issues were most keenly felt on landing in desert conditions, when dust clouds known as brown-outs caused by the helicopters rotors could temporarily blind pilots. Without a reserve of power, Lynx pilots had to carefully judge landings in dust clouds and many said that things could get interesting if anything unexpected occurred, such as the helicopter coming under fire. An Iraqi veteran Lynx pilot recalled 'on dusty landings when you were committed to landing, you were going to land. You have no power to overshoot.'

The power issue was only resolved when the Lynx AH.9A variant was introduced in 2009 with the uprated new LHTEC CTS800-4N engines and associated FADEC engine control system but this was too late for the Lynx crews serving in Operation Telic.

The formal role of the Lynx in southern Iraq also did not change much over the first four years of Operation Telic, although the different brigades that ran the British operation in Basra all put different emphasis on particular tactics and procedures.

Lynx detachments had to be ready to carry out five main roles during their time in Iraq. Firstly, they had to carry out airborne intelligence gathering of suspected insurgent hideouts or arms caches. This drew on many years experience in Northern Ireland and was usually conducted in co-operation with the Royal Artillery close observation battery in Basra, which provided photographers equipped with very long camera lenses to photograph targets of interest. It could also involve flying Intelligence Corps personnel to over-fly locations to enhance their understanding of the situation on the ground.

Flying top cover for re-supply convoys and infantry patrols was a big requirement and would see the Lynx fly up and down the ground units' route to look out for insurgent ambushes or teams planting improvised explosive devices (IED). A variation on this mission was the flying of airborne security patrols around desert landing strips being prepared for RAF Lockheed C-130 Hercules to bring in supplies.

Airborne fire support was another Lynx specialty, although the 7.62mm General Purpose Machine Gun (GPMG) door gun usually carried by the Lynx was often out-ranged in engagement with insurgents armed with big 12.7mm heavy machine guns. A more attractive proposition was embarking an army sniper in the back cabin who could be used to provide overwatch of high-value targets. This was very popular with ground commanders organizing raids or strike operations, against insurgent hideouts, giving them precision fire support from a high vantage point.

British strike operations in the backstreets of Basra were always plagued by radio communications problems because the large buildings interrupted the signals of the small radios used by British troops. To overcome this

The MX-15 thermal imaging camera systems, code-named Broadsword, transformed AAC operations from 2007. (Tim Ripley)

problem, the Lynx detachments regularly flew airborne rebroadcast missions to provide communications coverage during important operations.

Although weight and endurance were always an issue for the Lynx detachment in Iraq, it always stood ready to carry out the limited movement of men and material. This was particularly the case when critical items, such as spare parts for weapons and armoured vehicles, or radio equipment needed to be delivered to isolated British bases in a short space of time. The Lynx had in the past been used extensively as VIP transport, but in Iraq most senior officers and politicians usually were accompanied by such large retinues of staff officers and assistants that larger Westland Sea Kings or Pumas would be used to move them rather than the small Lynx.

A major enhancement of the Lynx role occurred in the spring of 2007, when the first AH.9 helicopters equipped with the L-3 Communications MX-15 thermal imaging camera system arrived in Iraq. Known as the Broadsword fit, these cameras had previously been installed in Royal Navy Sea King HC.4s of JHF(I). A similar system, known as the P4, had been fitted to RAF Pumas but it been plagued with technical problems and was no longer in use in southern Iraq by 2005.

A Broadsword mission console in a Royal Navy Sea King HC.4 helicopter. The same system was later installed in AAC Lynx AH.9 helicopters deployed to Basra. (Tim Ripley)

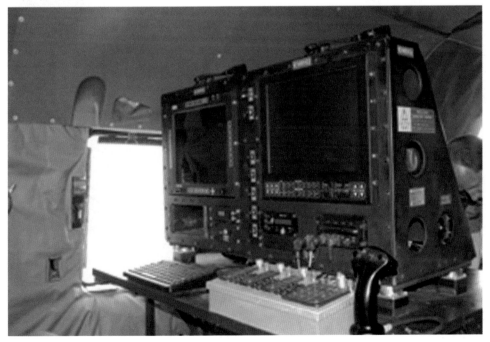

The Broadsword-equipped Sea Kings had been an instant hit with British troops because the video imagery they collected could be broadcast live to small laptop-sized video receiver terminals. For the first time very junior army commanders had access to live video imagery of targets that previously had only been available to senior commanders in remote headquarters. In the summer of 2005, when two British Special Air Service soldiers were captured by Iraqi militia fighters, a Broadsword Sea King kept them under surveillance during the period of their captivity and provided vital intelligence to allow a successful rescue to be organized.

By late 2006, the first L-3 Communications ROVER terminals were entering service with the British Army that allowed ground commanders to view imagery from multiple sources in a single receiver terminal. A simple dial allowed them to tune into whichever helicopter, aircraft or unmanned aerial vehicle was broadcasting imagery of their target.

The growing intensity of the war in Afghanistan in 2006, meant that the Broadsword Sea Kings were scheduled to be transferred to Helmand province in early 2007, so an urgent operational requirement (UOR) programme was launched to equip four Lynx AH.9s in Basra with Broadsword equipment. This was taken to Iraq in the spring of 2007 and was an immediate success.

Lynx AH.9 commanders could monitor imagery from the MX-15 cameras by means of a rugged tablet. (Tim Ripley)

An end of tour photo of a AAC detachment in Basra. Every AAC Lynx squadron served in Iraq between 2003 and 2009. (Basra Media Pool)

For the next two years it meant the Lynx detachment had a key intelligence, surveillance, targeting acquisition and reconnaissance (ISTAR) role in southern Iraq. Whenever a high priority operation was being planned or undertaken, the Lynx detachment was invariably in the thick of the action conducting pre-mission intelligence gathering or providing commanders with a real-time eye in the sky as the operation unfolded.

The MX-15 was relatively simple to use and reliable, making it far more popular than the P4 system it replaced. When fitted to the Lynx it allowed the stand-off targets to be observed at up to 6,000 metres while flying at heights that meant the helicopters could not be heard on the ground, giving it the ability to carry out covert surveillance of targets. The system comprised an externally mounted camera, a data link antenna mounted under the helicopter's tail boom and an operator station in the rear cabin. This was manned by the Lynx's Aviation Crewman and he could either select video imagery to be recorded for later analysis or download it in real time to a viewing terminal. There was also a tablet screen that allowed the helicopter's commander to view the imagery while he sat in the helicopter's front seat.

The MX-15 and Lynx combination proved very popular because it gave ground commanders a similar imagery to that provided by unmanned aerial vehicles but the Lynx also brought with it a door-mounted 7.62mm GPMG for offensive action and in extreme situations the helicopter could land and pick up casualties or move small group of troops around the battlefield.

As the campaign in southern Iraq unfolded the role of the Lynx detachment evolved considerably. When the first post-war Lynx squadron arrived at Basra in July 2003, the main pre-occupation of the British garrison was trying to restore power, water and all the other public utilities essential to returning the city to some semblance of normality. Looting and sabotage meant the British started to use their four Lynx AH.7s and four Gazelle AH.1 helicopters to fly surveillance and deterrence patrols to protect key pieces of civilian infrastructure. By the autumn, British troops were coming under increasing attacks by insurgents and JHF(I) was augmented by three additional Gazelles equipped with Ultra 4000 cameras and two RAF Pumas with P4 thermal cameras for ISTAR tasks.

The spring of 2004 saw southern Iraq convulsed by the so-called Sadr revolt after militia fighters loyal to the Shia cleric Muqtada al-Sadr and his Jaysh al-Mahdi militia. British bases across the region were attacked and the base in the town of Al Amarah in the centre of Maysan province was besieged for several months. The upsurge in fighting was bad news for the Gazelle after its defensive systems were found wanting and the type had to be pulled out of Iraq by the summer.

The British battlegroup in Maysan was reinforced to drive back the militia and this included the detachment of a pair of Lynx to Camp Abu Naji on the outskirts of Al Amarah. They were in the thick of the action flying reconnaissance and support missions for the beleaguered British force. For the next two years, the Lynx detachment continued to split its effort between Basra airbase and Al Amarah. There was a brief interlude in November and December 2004 when the Black Watch battlegroup deployed north to near Fallujah to help US forces during their assault on the insurgent held city. During Operation Bracken, 652 Squadron detached a Lynx AH.9 for a week at a time to support the Black Watch. The Lynx worked as part of an aviation detachment with an RAF Puma moving passengers, evacuating casualties and conducting surveillance. The Black Watch commanding officer, Lieutenant Colonel James Cowan, wrote in his post operational tour report:

> Helicopters greatly enhanced operational capability and were used extensively throughout the period of their deployment on Op Bracken. Surveillance, aerial security following incidents, deployment of an air reaction force and logistic runs were the most important tasks. There is no doubt that their presence saved lives.

In the summer of 2006, the British commander in Basra decided to pull back the troops from Al Amarah to concentrate his resources in the city to launch a major drive, code-named Operation Sinbad, to push out the militia. Trouble had been escalating in the city for several months as Sadr's militia tried to seize control of key buildings and districts. In May 2006, they brought down an 847 Squadron Lynx with a manportable surface-to-air missile over central Basra, killing all five British personnel on board, including an AAC exchange pilot. The event was a major challenge to British air supremacy over Basra. Helicopter flights over Basra city in daylight had to be curtailed except in exceptional circumstances. Work was also begun to enhance defensive systems on the Lynx. The arrival of MX-15 in early 2007 put the Lynx back in the ISTAR game over Basra and allowed it to carry out stand-off surveillance of urban targets without bringing the helicopter into range of militia heavy weapons.

Over the next year, British forces began pulling out of bases throughout Basra as part of the London government's policy of handing over security

RAF Merlin HC.3 support helicopters served in Basra alongside the AAC from 2005 to 2009. (AgustaWestland)

The Lynx AH.9 was the mainstay of the AAC in southern Iraq between 2007 to 2009. (AgustaWestland)

responsibility to Iraq forces. To many in Basra this seemed like a retreat in the face of growing insurgent attacks and a fatal sign of weakness that only seemed to embolden the militia.

During the spring and summer, British troops began concentrating their forces at Basra airport, now rebranded as the Contingency Operating Base or COB. It now became the focus for militia attacks and through the summer was receiving some seventy rocket and mortar attacks a month. This barrage led the RAF to pull its AgustaWestland Merlin HC.3 transport helicopters back to a safer base in northern Kuwait. The AAC Lynx detachment stayed put and its personnel became used to taking cover whenever the rocket alarm sounded.

This situation was turned around in March 2008 when Iraqi troops arrived from Baghdad and launched an offensive against the militia fighters who now controlled most of Basra. Operation Charge of the Knights soon involved British troops in a supporting role and the Lynx of 672 Squadron were heavily involved in ISTAR operations or moving personnel around the city.

By the end of the year the British government had decided to wind down its military commitment in Iraq. Troops of 20 Armoured Brigade wound up Operation Telic on 30 April 2009. 659 Squadron spent another month

126

flying security missions for Operation Brockdale as the mission to remove all the British Army's vehicles and equipment from Basra to ports in Kuwait was code-named. Then it was time for it to dismantle its helicopters, ready for them to be loaded on trucks and driven through the desert to Kuwait. The last Lynx sortie was flown in on 25 May 2009, after some 1,800 sorties and 2,300 flying hours had been completed, burning some 11,500kg of aviation fuel.

Operation Telic was perhaps one of the highpoints of the AAC career of the Lynx. The deployment of the Lynx, particularly after the installation of the MX-15 in 2007, proved the usefulness of light utility helicopters and helped win many of the arguments in the run up to the formal launching of the Future Lynx or Wildcat project, as well as in subsequent defence reviews when the project appeared to be under threat.

Chapter 9

British Army UAVs against Iraq Insurgency, 2003 to 2009

A Royal Artillery Desert Hawk troop commander in 9 Battery, 12 Regiment Royal Artillery, recalled in the *Gunner* journal:

> The main tasking of 9 Battery was supporting the RAF Regiment as they conducted base defence patrols [around Basra airbase]. Over flying routes and patrols were our tasks, but in addition we provided intimate support to the patrols, reacting instantly to any change in the situation.

He continued:

> Desert Hawk can look into areas out of sight of patrolling soldiers, and patrol commanders are able to view images of what is going on in areas of dead ground via a live feed into a vehicle borne terminal.' It was very popular. As our experience grew we became very familiar with the ground and could usually forecast where each patrol was going, enabling us to check for enemy activity at pre-designated areas of interest along their probable route.

The summer and autumn of 2003 saw the Iraqi insurgency that started around the Middle East country's capital spreading to the British Army area of responsibility around Basra. The Royal Artillery officer's comments make clear that the role of UAVs in counter-insurgency operations were very different from those required in full-blown war fighting.

British troops were being regularly ambushed and their bases were coming under mortar and gun attack. Sabotage attacks against civilian infrastructure made it difficult for British troops to help the local population, creating a vicious circle of collapsing confidence and support for international forces across the country.

Plans were put in hand to enhance the size and capabilities of the British division in southern Iraq and it came as no surprise that 32nd Regiment and its Phoenix UAVs would be heading to Basra when the next troop rotation took place in the late autumn of 2003. This time the regiment would deploy a battery-sized force to provide ISTAR support the UK-led Multi-National Division South East (MND SE) across the four provinces of southern Iraq, where British troops were responsible for security.

57 Battery started deploying in October 2003 and by the middle of November its Phoenix air vehicles were flying daily missions across southern Iraq from the unit's main base, a Shaibah logistic base, to the south-west of Basra. Phoenix missions were flown mainly at night to patrol along power lines, water and oil pipes to prevent insurgent sabotage, as well as around British bases to give warning of insurgent attacks. Intelligence-gathering missions were also flown to try to head-off suspected insurgent attacks.

Basra as seen through the night vision camera of a Phoenix unmanned aerial vehicle. (BAE Systems)

In the spring of 2004, 57 Battery handed over to 22 Battery, which took over the operation of Phoenix and brought with it the British Army's newest UAV, the Lockheed Martin Desert Hawk I. The hand-over of batteries coincided with the outbreak of the so-called Sadr revolt, which saw radical Shia militia men launch sustained attacks against British bases across southern Iraq.

The Phoenix was in its element, providing an eye-in-the-sky for beleaguered British troops across Iraq. During the first months of the British occupation of southern Iraq, Phoenix operations were largely reactive in nature, with regular missions being flown to watch over power lines and oil pipelines to prevent sabotage, as well as patrolling the perimeters of British bases to alert the occupants of approaching insurgents. As British troops started to gain a better understanding of the insurgent groups, the Phoenix was used to monitor suspected insurgent safe houses and supply routes and provide what was termed 'overwatch' of raids or strike operations to apprehend insurgents. Flight safety restrictions, however, prevented the Phoenix from flying over the centre of Basra city.

The deployment of the hand-launched Desert Hawk was less of a success because the radio downlink that controlled the air vehicle and transmitted live video imagery suffered from interference from the newly established Iraqi civilian mobile phone network. The commander of British forces in Iraq, Major General Andrew Stewart, was not impressed and described the Desert Hawk as a 'joke' in his post tour report. The General said Phoenix gave good support up until April when the summer heat started to impact on its performance. This led Phoenix operations to wind down and by July most big UAV air vehicles and launcher equipment was placed in storage in the rapidly expanding Shaibah base.

18 Battery returned to Iraq in October 2004 to re-activate the Phoenix capability. It began expanding its area of operations deploying flight troops to Al Amarah in support of the Welsh Guards and Camp Smitty out on the border with Saudi Arabia in support of Dutch troops. The battery had a very successful tour, flying 125 missions at a success rate of 96 per cent; the lowest-ever failure rate for Phoenix operations. The operation was also notable for the excellent tactical integration of UAVs with ground troops. The Welsh Guards battlegroup refined the use of UAVs in providing top cover to mobile patrols and the Phoenix was subsequently credited with being a major factor in deterring insurgent attacks on UK forces around Al Amarah, as well as greatly improving the understanding of the pattern of life of the local population. The battery also achieved considerable success in queuing Dutch Apache attack helicopters to interdict insurgents on the Iraqi-Saudi border. The battery suffered no casualties and returned to Robert's Barracks in Larkhill in March 2005.

32nd Regiment's batteries were now settled into a schedule of rotations out to Basra to support the British contingent, which was increasingly embattled as the insurgency continued to escalate. Each battery usually deployed with two launcher troops, each of three launch vehicles, and two Tac Groups equipped with a ground control station and ground data terminal so they deployed to an infantry battlegroup headquarters and provided the commander with imagery. At any one time a Tac Group and Launcher troop were grouped into what was termed the Lead Flight Troop Group, held at very short notice to deploy around southern Iraq as the tactical situation required. The growing threat of insurgent improvised explosive devices (IEDs) meant that the British divisional command in southern Iraq had to take great care in deciding to commit the Lead Flight Troop Group, which had unarmoured vehicles, to operations away from the safety of Shaibah Logistic Base, where the main battery was based.

Royal Artillery personnel prepare a Phoenix unmanned aerial vehicle for mission over southern Iraq. (Private Collection)

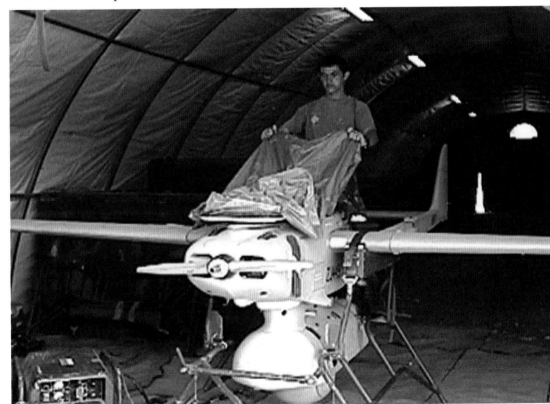

Royal Artillery Unmanned Aerial Vehicle Battery Deployments to Iraq, 2003 to 2009, Operation Telic

Tour date	Battery	Equipment
Jan to Jun 03	RHQ 32nd Regiment RA	Phoenix
Jan to Jun 03	22 (Gibraltar 1779–1783) Battery	Phoenix
Jan to Jun 03	18 (Quebec 1759) Battery	Phoenix
Nov 03 to Feb 04	57 (Bhurtpore 1825–1826) Battery	Phoenix
Mar to Sept 04	22 (Gibraltar 1779–1783) Battery	Phoenix & Desert Hawk I
Oct 04 to Mar 05	18 (Quebec 1759) Battery	Phoenix
Mar to Jul 05	42 (Alem Hamza) Battery	Phoenix & Desert Hawk I
Aug 05 to Jan 06	57 (Bhurtpore 1825–1826) Battery	Phoenix & Desert Hawk I
Oct 05 to Nov 05	18 (Quebec 1759) Battery	Phoenix
Feb to Jun 06	18 (Quebec 1759) Battery	Phoenix
May to Nov 07	22 (Gibraltar 1779–1783) Battery	Hermes 450 & Desert Hawk III
Nov 07 to Apr 08	18 (Quebec 1759) Battery	Hermes 450
Nov 07 to Apr 08	21 (Air Assault) Battery	Desert Hawk III
Apr to Oct 08	42 (Alem Hamza) Battery	Hermes 450
Apr to Oct 08	25/170 (Imjin) Battery	Desert Hawk III
Oct 08 to Apr 09	57 (Bhurtpore 1825–1826) Battery	Hermes 450
Oct 08 to Apr 09	10 (Assaye) Battery	Desert Hawk III
Apr to June 09	22 (Gibraltar 1779–1783) Battery	Hermes 450
Apr to June 09	9 (Plassey) Battery	Desert Hawk III

The focus of the Phoenix batteries activity increasingly became Al Amarah where the British contingent in the city was under daily attack from large numbers of well-armed insurgents. During late 2005 and into 2006, 57 Battery's flight troop at Al Amarah flew some sixty missions. The detachment encountered the worst mortar and rocket barrage experienced in southern Iraq since 2003. One 32nd Regiment soldier was injured by flying shrapnel in that attack and was returned to the UK to recover.

A senior office with 57 Battery during this tour, said different British battlegroups and brigades were much better than others at using Phoenix to best effect. He said:

> The best ones were those that are forward thinking, imaginative and open minded. Flying UAVs is a means to achieve an end – right sensor, right place, right time to achieve the right effect. Supported battlegroups need to think system of systems and avoid tasking Phoenix in isolation.

He said the use of the Phoenix had evolved considerably from its old role of spotting targets for artillery. Missions included deterrence – the insurgents did not know what Phoenix could do and could not see it. This kept them guessing about what the Phoenix was doing when they hear it overhead. In turn, this reassured British troops and the local population.

By early June 2006 the temperatures had reached over 40°C – two degrees higher than the system operating limit – and it was time for the Phoenix to return to the UK but the system was not going to return to Iraq. The intensive use of the air vehicles meant that 32nd Regiment was running out of them. By September 2005 there were only eighty-four air vehicles left in the British Army's inventory and it was then predicted that half would be lost by the end of 2008. Drastic restrictions on the use of the Phoenix were imposed a year earlier but the situation in southern Iraq meant that any that crashed could not be recovered and repaired. The commanding officer of 32nd Regiment had to issue a directive to his battery in Iraq, saying:

> You are to ensure that supported operational commanders, and staff, are aware of the limited number of Phoenix UAV available to support current and future operations. UAVs are not to be flown as a matter of routine, but where and when the operational imperative merits their use, recognizing the risk of aircraft damage that may result from the task, and remaining cognisant of the requirement to protect the stock of aircraft.

In 2005 batteries were restricted to taking forty Phoenix air vehicles with them on six-month tours to Iraq but even with the tight restrictions on flying the loss rate was just too high for the limited stock. The deteriorating security situation in Iraq made it increasingly difficult to recover damage aircraft for repair because of the risk to troops of ambush by insurgents, but this was just at the time front-line commanders wanted Phoenix missions to be surged. The time was up for Phoenix after less than a decade in formal British Army service and in 2006 there were just not enough air vehicles left to sustain a viable operational detachment in Iraq. It was decided that the system would remain in use for training in the UK and be officially retired in March 2008.

22 Battery was the last Phoenix battery deployed to support Operation Telic. The final operational flight of the Phoenix was conducted by Koehler's Troop in May 2006, at Camp Abu Naji near Al Amarah. The battery finally returned home in mid-June 2006 but left behind the newly formed Imagery Downlink Group (IDG) consisting of a captain, a sergeant and two Gunners in Basra. The IDG proved an important pointer to the future of British UAV operations. It used some of the first full-motion video receivers that allowed group troops to view in real time video from both UAVs, helicopters and aircraft equipped with thermal-imaging cameras. This laptop-

Map 8-1 Iraq in 2003. (CIA)

sized equipment allowed troops serving in combat to watch video and revolutionized UAV operations, putting imagery directly in the hands of front-line troops for the first time, rather than restricting access to imagery to senior commanders at high-level headquarters. The IDG remained in Iraq until the beginning of August 2006, just in time to see the long-awaited

134

The first versions of the Desert Hawk suffered serious technical problems during their missions over southern Iraq in 2004. (Private collection)

arrival of the new American-made L-3 Communications ROVER 3 terminal, which was the first terminal that could receive imagery from more than one type of aircraft, UAV or helicopter. From 2005 on wards 32nd Regiment's Tac Groups were increasingly equipped with video imagery receivers and this would have a profound effect on how the British Army used UAVs. But up until the arrival of ROVER terminals they had to operate three different terminals to watch imagery from American and Italian General Atomics MQ-1 Predator UAVs, RAF Nimrod MR2 maritime patrol aircraft with the MX-15 camera and Longhorn II data link and Royal Navy Westland Sea King HC.2s with the MX-15 'Broadsword' camera systems.

The departure of the Phoenix from Iraq in 2006 left a major gap in the intelligence, surveillance, targeting and reconnaissance (ISTAR) capability of the British-led division in southern Iraq. The Desert Hawk had been modified to overcome the interference problem with the mobile phone network but it was only able to operate close to British bases for an hour at a time and its imagery could not be distributed beyond the small laptop-sized control unit. As a result the Desert Hawk was used almost exclusively to provide perimeter

135

surveillance of British bases. Support for offensive strike operations largely fell to the Broadsword-equipped Sea King HC.4 helicopters of the Royal Navy.

The RAF Regiment loaned a small number AeroVironment RQ-11 Raven mini UAVs from the US Army in the autumn of 2006 to help its airfield defence squadron in Basra protect the city's airbase. The British Army conducted a couple of trials in southern Iraq. The Queen's Royal Hussars took a Raven system out into the desert around Al Amarah for one of these trials but when it flew into an RAF AgustaWestland Merlin HC.3 helicopter parked next to their camp the watching group of senior officers were less than impressed and the Raven remained as a RAF Regiment system.

It was also hoped that the increase of RAF personnel assigned to the USAF Predator Task Force would result in an increase in availability of the American UAV to British forces in Basra but Baghdad remained a priority for the USAF and the British Army had no certainty of when the Predator would be supporting them.

The first Hermes 450 unmanned aerial vehicles made their combat debut over Iraq in June 2007. (Thales)

The then commander of British forces in Basra, Major General Richard Shirreff, was exasperated at the failure of the Ministry of Defence in London to generate a replacement for the Phoenix. He later told the Chilcot inquiry into the Iraq war that:

> ... it beggared belief that nearly three and a half years after the start of this campaign, we still [had] no UAV capable of flying in south-east Iraq, in the summer. I was told that no more staff effort could possibly be put in to deploying UAVs to south-east Iraq. I think [this was] just because the Ministry of Defence was incapable of generating the drive and energy to deliver them.

The problem revolved around the contract for the replacement for the Phoenix, the Watchkeeper, which was signed with the French defence company Thales in July 2005. Only enough money could be found by the Treasury (finance ministry) to fund a slow rate of development to allow

Basra International Airport was home to a Royal Artillery Hermes 450 battery from 2007 to 2009. (Thales)

delivery of the Watchkeeper to the British Army in 2010. Thales had offered to lease an interim solution, based around the Hermes 450 UAV, which the Watchkeeper was to be evolved from, to cover any gap if the Phoenix had to be withdrawn from service early. This was turned down on cost grounds by the Treasury and Ministry of Defence. The British government at this point still believed that events in Iraq were moving in a positive direction and the UK garrison could be reduced from its divisional strength to a battalion-sized force by 2006. In this environment there was no appetite to spend large amounts of money on new equipment that would only be used for a few months. Inflexible Treasury urgent operational requirement (UOR) rules also meant that money could not be spent on equipment that could be used outside operational theatres to replace in-service equipment in the long term.

Events in Iraq and Afghanistan during the summer and autumn of 2006 would turn this situation around. The rosy scenario for Iraq and Afghanistan disappeared as British troops in Basra and Helmand province found themselves almost under siege in their bases. The public mood shifted under a spate of media reports that British troops lacked the equipment needed to fight and win. In September 2006, an RAF Nimrod MR2 crashed in

The Hermes 450 transformed British surveillance capabilities in southern Iraq. (Thales)

Afghanistan and immediately the aircraft, which provided a great deal of the UK full motion video surveillance capability, was grounded for prolonged periods as safety problems were rectified.

By the end of 2006, new UOR funding was agreed for new UAVs for Iraq and Afghanistan. New batches of Desert Hawk III variants were ordered and a replacement for the Phoenix was finally agreed. Thales was asked to dust off its plans to provide Hermes 450 systems. In only six months, lease contracts were signed, crews trained and hardware was delivered to Basra airbase.

22 Battery returned to Basra in the spring of 2007 with the new Desert Hawks and in June its first Hermes 450s became operational. The Hermes 450 was several generations in advance of the venerable Phoenix. It had four times the endurance on station, was far more airworthy and unlike the Phoenix could be safely flown over Iraqi towns and cities. Whereas a whole Phoenix battery was lucky to fly some 500 hours during a six-month tour in Iraq, a single

The fourteen-hour plus endurance of the Hermes 450 unmanned aerial vehicle meant targets in southern Iraqi could be kept under near continuous surveillance. (Thales)

Hermes 450 could run up that many flight hours in a month of operations. The new UAV's sensors had longer range and generated far sharper images that allowed intelligence analysts to even identify the type of small arms being carried by insurgents. Crucially, the imagery from the Hermes 450 could be downloaded directly into remote viewing terminals so front-line troops could watch the imagery in real time. At first a bespoke receiver was in use but by the end of 2007 Hermes 450 imagery could be received by the L-3 Communications ROVER terminals that were becoming standard issue across the US and British armed forces.

The British UAV force in Iraq was now put on a firm footing with 32nd Regiment providing half a battery's worth of personnel, around fifty troops, to run the Hermes 450 detachment and the responsibility for manning the Desert Hawk fell to air defence troops from 47th Regiment Royal Artillery, who were temporarily re-roled as mini-UAV operators. The balance of each battery's personnel operated UAVs in Afghanistan.

Within days of the arrival, the Hermes 450 and Desert Hawk III crews of 22 Battery were in the thick of the action helping to protect British bases under siege in downtown Basra. A Desert Hawk detachment was embedded with the 4th Battalion, The Rifles (4 Rifles), inside the Basra Palace base, on the southern edge of the city. Militia fighters were becoming increasingly emboldened and were launching hourly mortar, rocket and small arms attacks on the base. Accordingly the battlegroup commander, Lieutenant Colonel Patrick Saunders, said that during the summer his troops were on the receiving end of 1,800 mortar and stand-off rocket rounds, 85 IED attacks, 250 rocket-propelled grenades and so much small arms fire they stopped counting. The Desert Hawk and Hermes 450 were the only way the Colonel Saunders' beleaguered troops could safely look outside their base to try to get an idea of what was happening in the city, which was now almost totally under the control of radical Shia militia groups. The Hermes 450 and Desert Hawk were at this point providing 90 per cent of all full-motion video imagery downloaded by British troops in southern Iraq.

The autumn of 2007 saw the withdrawal of the last British troops from central Basra out to the airport after senior commanders struck a deal with militia leaders. British UAVs were airborne continuously in the run-up to the final withdrawal from the Basra Palace to monitor the route back to the airport to ensure no improvised explosive devices were planted that might threaten the withdrawal.

The final withdrawal of troops from the 4 Rifles battlegroup went off without a shot being fired and nervous commanders at the British head-quarter at Basra airport followed the column's progress by a video feed from a Hermes 450.

The other major task of 22 Battery was to monitor the desert around the Basra airbase – now renamed the Contingency Operating Base (COB) – for insurgent mortar and rocket teams. Up until British troops pulled out of Basra Palace, the airbase was attacked on a daily basis with seventy-four strikes taking place in July alone. The Royal Artillery deployed a warning and counter-battery force to the airport to take on the militia indirect fire (IDF) teams. By the summer of 2007, IDF was the main cause of casualties among the British Army in Iraq. Mamba and Cobra locating radars provided around-the-clock surveillance around the COB and when they tracked an incoming round a UAV would be despatched to provide a positive visual identification, to allow a 105mm or 155mm artillery fire to be brought down in the IDF team. The Royal Artillery claimed they could close the 'find-fix-destroy loop' in a matter of minutes but the attacks continued on the COB for the rest of 2007, although at a much lower intensity.

A stalemate of sorts existed until March 2008, when Iraqi troops sent by the Baghdad government arrived in Basra with the mission to drive out the militias. Now 18 Battery, which replaced 22 Battery in December 2007, was

Launch and recover, as well as maintenance support of Hermes 450s was carried out by civilian contractors. (Thales)

well poised to play a key role in Operation Charge of the Knights, as the Iraqi offensive was dubbed, flying missions to find insurgents in the back streets of Basra. US, British and Iraqi troops leading the offensive could download the Hermes 450 imagery and help them see what was around street corners and behind buildings.

Faced with overwhelming and well-aimed firepower, the militias were soon in retreat and the situation in Basra was transformed. Iraqi and coalition troops were able to restore control of the city and life returned to some sort of normality for the first time in six years.

32nd and 47th Regiment, assisted briefly by 9 Battery from 12th Regiment Royal Artillery, remained on duty in Iraq until 11 May 2009 providing top cover for the British contingent as it prepared to end Operation Telic. The last missions by 32nd Regiment ended just over six years of almost continuous operations in Iraq.

British Army UAVs operations in Iraq were transformed during the six years of the occupation mission. The first four years of Operation Telic demonstrated the limitations of the British Army's UAVs but once modern systems were acquired in 2007, UAV operations moved forward at a rapid pace.

Chapter 10

Into Afghanistan –
Operation Herrick, 2006 to 2007

When the news emerged in January 2007 that four British Royal Marines and soldiers had strapped themselves onto the outside of two Agusta-Westland Apache AH.1 attack helicopters and been flown into an enemy territory in southern Afghanistan to rescue a missing Royal Marine it was greeted with incredulity. This was bravery of the highest order and left many wondering why one participant won the Distinguished Flying Cross and three received the Military Cross for their part in the rescue, rather than the country's highest bravery decoration, the Victoria Cross.

The mission commander, Warrant Officer Class 1 Tom O'Malley, received the DFC. Warrant Officer Class 1 Ed Macy and Staff Sergeant Keith Armatage, both Army Air Corps, along with Captain David Rigg Royal Engineers, all received the British armed forces' third highest decoration for gallantry for their part in the rescue of the body of Lance Corporal Mathew Ford. Macey and Armitage's medal citations need little embellishment.

On 15 January 2007 Macy and Armatage were the Apache pilots supporting a raid into a Taliban stronghold. Despite a heavy preparatory air and artillery bombardment, the ground assault had resulted in five British casualties around the walls of the fort. Following the confusion of the withdrawal one of the casualties, Lance Corporal Ford, was reported missing in action. A plan to rescue him was made.

Macy demonstrated selfless gallantry and leadership as he helped inspire a hastily drawn together team to recover Ford. Macy's courage, quick thinking and determination to find and recover Ford, with complete disregard for his own safety were an outstanding act of valour and leadership.

During the mission to recover Ford's body Armatage was unable to land [his helicopter] where planned. The rescuers were disorientated and, seeing this, Armatage armed only with a pistol, got out of his aircraft to lead them to the casualty. Almost immediately, they came under enemy small arms fire. Throughout this audacious mission, Armatage's flying was impressively courageous and skilful. However, the fact that he evacuated his Apache armed only with a pistol to bring coherence to Ford's recovery was truly extraordinary.

Rigg, despite thinking he was about to be thrown into a deliberate enemy ambush, volunteered immediately to take part in the rescue of Ford [strapping himself to the outside of an Apache]. He knew that he would be returning to face an aggressive, determined and lethal enemy, who were already alert to the company's presence and were very likely to anticipate their return to find Ford. In the ensuing action Rigg displayed outstanding valour, clarity of thought and purpose to recover Ford and return him to his comrades, in the face of a lethal and determined enemy, with deliberate disregard for his own safety.

The dramatic rescue mission into Jugroom Fort in 2007 saw AAC helicopter crews awarded decorations for valour. (Kandahar Media Pool)

Over the summer of 2006 and into 2007, the Apache AH.1 crews of 9 Regiment AAC were in action on a daily basis helping to protect isolated detachments of British Paratroopers and Royal Marines in Helmand province. These battles have entered military folklore as time after time, the arrival of pairs of Apache would save the day by driving off hundreds of Taliban fighters besieging the British bases.

Since then the AAC has seen extensive action in Afghanistan more than proving the value of large investment in the fleet of sixty-seven Apache and the continued utility of the Lynx. The Attack Helicopter (AH) Force has been involved in a wide range of operations in Afghanistan, ranging from close air support, deep strike missions, escort, surveillance and reconnaissance.

The Dishforth-based 9 Regiment AAC had been preparing for its Afghan mission since the spring of 2005 when the then Defence Secretary Dr John

ACC Apache AH.1 attach helicopters arrived at Kandahar Airfield in southern Afghanistan in May 2006. (Tim Ripley)

The desert of southern Afghanistan provided little cover for the Taliban to hide from prowling AAC Apache AH.1s. (AgustaWestland)

Reid approved plans to deploy the regiment's Apache as part of the expanded British force, based on 16 Air Assault Brigade, in the central Asian country. Intense preparation and training began in the wake of Exercise Eagle Strike in May 2005, which formally declared 9 Regiment as combat ready, as the UK Lead Aviation Task Force. Alongside the Apache, four Westland Lynx AH.7s of 672 Squadron were designated to deploy to Afghanistan. They were intended to provide mobility for senior commanders, armed overwatch of supply convoy movements, radio rebroadcast, casualty evacuation and limited cargo movement.

The culmination of this training package occurred in April 2006 when 3rd Battalion, the Parachute Regiment (3 PARA) and 9 Regiment AAC were flown to Oman for a huge live-firing exercise. This put the Apache to the test for the first time in desert conditions and allowed the Royal Electrical and Mechanical Engineers (REME) to develop a fix to clean out sand and so prevent jamming of the helicopter's 30mm cannons.

146

The Afghan operation saw the creation of a unique British aviation unit that combined attack, transport and observation helicopters under a single commander. Dubbed Joint Helicopter Force (Afghanistan) (JHF(A)), it provided the UK Task Force with a powerful rotary wing force to conduct combat operations, fly resupply and casualty evacuations. For the AAC it meant that Afghanistan would not see the deployment of an aviation battlegroup.

The JHF(A) had its headquarters at Kandahar airfield and provided helicopters to work under the tactical command of the 3 PARA battlegroup at Camp Bastion. On each day during the summer of 2006, JHF(A) had to provide basic casualty evacuation and medical coverage for the British force

NATO in Afghanistan in 2006. (NATO)

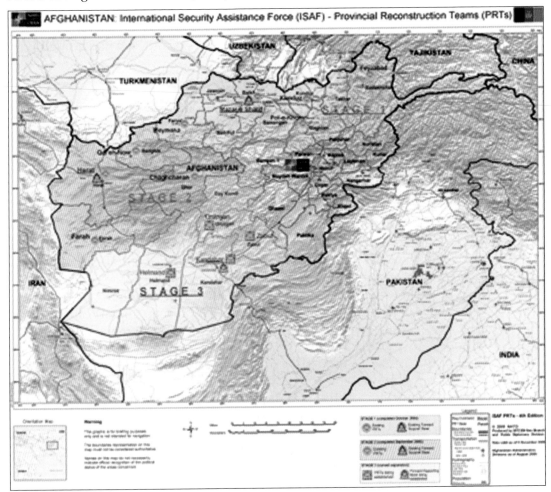

and a reserve or reaction force element to respond to unforeseen events such as a helicopter crash. Any extra capacity could be made available for deliberate or pre-planned British operations. Other NATO nations and the Afghans could also request British helicopter support.

RAF and AAC officers took turns to lead JHF(A) with the commanding officer of 9 Regiment AAC, Lieutenant Colonel Richard Felton, running it during the summer of 2006 before handing over to a RAF Wing Commander from the Chinook force.

A flavour of the fighting in the summer of 2006 was provided by a an RAF flight lieutenant who flew Boeing Chinook HC.2s in Helmand during this period.

> On a typical day, two Apache and two Chinook were deployed with the Immediate Reaction [medical] Team (IRT) and the [platoon-sized] Helmand Reaction Force (HRF) on stand-by at Bastion, 24/7. IRT/HRF were our priority and had to be sustained. They brought out wounded troops and responded to crisis.

Lieutenant Colonel Richard Felton led 9 Regiment AAC into Afghanistan in 2006 in the first operational deployment of the UK's Apache force. (Tim Ripley)

Joint operations with RAF Chinook HC.2 support helicopters to deliver assault troops deep into enemy territory soon became a regular feature of AAC Apache AH.1 operations in Afghanistan. (Canadian Ministry of National Defence)

An AAC Apache AH.1 pilot recalled:

> We used Kandahar as our maintenance area and the remainder of our force was based [at Bastion]. Of our eight aircraft, four were up at Bastion at any one time. The Apache main effort was forward [at Bastion].
>
> The threat determined that we had to work as a team. The Chinook was the army's life line but because of the threat and the fact that Apache provide fire support and eyes on target with its sensors we did joint-planning and preparation. You couldn't do it separately. To have any effect we worked closely as a team.

The Chinook pilot reinforced this point, '… working with Apache was routine. There was no RAF/army divide here. We just have different types of aircraft. We planned and briefed together.'

The first combat mission by 9 Regiment's Apache AH.1 was flown in May 2006 by a pair of AAC Apache, which were ordered into action near the Afghan town of Kajaki. The mission to destroy French special forces vehicles captured by Taliban insurgents was over in a matter of minutes after AGM-114 Hellfire missiles demolished the vehicles.

The AAC's Apache force was in action around the clock during the summer of 2006 as British troops found themselves besieged in Platoon Houses. (Tim Ripley)

The first phase of the Taliban offensive was against a small contingent of French and US Special Forces training ANA troops near the Kajaki Dam in the far north of Helmand province. Fear of the sudden arrival of hundreds of Taliban led the handful of Frenchmen and Americans to form up their Afghan allies in a convoy of trucks and head south to the NATO base outside Sangin on 20 May. The convoy had barely gone a few miles when it was ambushed. Hundreds of Taliban and their local allies subjected the convoy to a sustained attack over several dozen miles of road. Heavy fire broke up the convoy and the Frenchmen, along with dozens of Afghans, were isolated. Their unarmoured pick-up trucks and jeeps were riddled with bullets. The Americans had armoured Humvees and were able to escape to Forward Operating Base (FOB) Robinson. Later the remnants of the convoy limped into the base, leaving behind two dead Frenchmen and fifteen Afghans. A Company of 3 PARA was scrambled from Camp Bastion in Chinooks, escorted by Apache AH.1s, to try to search for missing Frenchmen and ANA troops. The Apache squadron had only just got up and running and was in the process of making its final Hellfire missile qualification firings when the call to Kajaki came. This was the first combat mission of the UK Apache force.

The Paratroopers found the abandoned vehicles and an AAC Apache AH.1 was called up to destroy one of the French jeeps to stop its highly secret position-tracking equipment falling into Taliban hands. It later emerged the local villagers had joined the ambush and helped mutilate the bodies. News of the Taliban 'victory' spread quickly.

With British and NATO road convoys still liable to be ambushed or hit with improvised explosive devices, the safest way to resupply the troops in the district centres and bring out wounded was by helicopter. This was not as easy as it seemed. The district centres were in the centre of urban areas and they did not have room inside them for helicopter landing sites, so it was not possible to land the big Chinooks safely inside them. The British troops had to mount patrols out of the district centres on to open ground to secure landing sites for any in-bound helicopters. This meant every helicopter mission into the district centres was high risk for both the grounds troops and helicopter crews alike. Often only the presence of Apache gunships circling above the landing sites allowed the Chinooks to get in and out safely.

A small detachment of Lynx AH.7s supported the British Task Force in Helmand province in 2006 flying surveillance, overwatch and liaison tasks. (Tim Ripley)

For senior British commanders it meant the nature of their operation in Helmand had fundamentally changed. Any idea of trying to conduct reconstruction or humanitarian operations was gone.

The bulk of the HTF's combat troops were committed in the district centre and were fighting for their lives. With the summer heat pushing above 50 degrees, food and water scarce and the troops fighting around the clock, senior officers wondered how long their men could keep fighting. Without the Chinooks and Apache bringing in supplies, or protecting road convoys, the troops would not have been able to hold on.

Brigadier Ed Butler, commander of 16 Air Assault Brigade, said 3 PARA could not have held out without the efforts of the RAF Chinook crews.

> They carried the most risk of anyone here – they can have 40 to 50 guys on board their helicopters. I must praise them for keeping going back, it was pretty close at times. They have done some awesome flying.

By moving his troops by air, the Brigadier said the Chinooks 'saved many lives'.

Towards the end of July, the supply situation was getting desperate so a series of battalion-sized deliberate operations were conducted around the district compounds to allow road convoys to get into the beleaguered troops. The bulk of the British Chinook and Apache force were massed for these operations to saturate the local area with more than 400 troops at a time. The first operation around Sangin in mid-July involved two companies of Paratroopers, with lavish air support, so the Taliban kept out of the way long enough for a large supply convoy to get into the district centre. Similar events followed in Now Zad and Musa Qalah over the next four weeks. These temporarily relieved the situation but the troops in the district centres were still calling up daily Apache and fixed-wing air strikes to neutralize Taliban rocket and mortar positions.

When the UK helicopters were concentrated for a deliberate operation, considerable planning and preparation were involved over a forty-eight-hour period. An AAC Captain who was an Apache AH.1 pilot who served in Helmand in the summer of 2006 said:

> There was massive co-ordination of the many moving parts, not just aviation. We used fast jet in support because we were the Airborne Forward Air Controllers in the fight. During deliberate operations we would talk in fast jets, monitoring the territory as the Chinook land.

He continues:

> We were busy but it ebbed and flowed. In general our tactics were very different from the Chinooks, they had to go to lower levels but there was still the RPG threat and terrain [problems]. The enemy usually knew we were coming so we were always evolving our tactics. Ideas were always coming from the ground troops on better ways to flush out the enemy. Finding them in the first place was most the difficult thing. This was very small scale stuff but highly dangerous.

The Chinook pilot said:

> Things were constantly changing, what you expect would not happen. Big multi-ship operations were hairy. The locals expected us and so you had to do it fast. There was a real risk. You needed speed. We had a few hits when we had to go in and land. The Apache stayed in the overhead but we had to descend into the threat area.

Apache crews said they only used close-in fire support (CIFS) procedures under the direct control of Paratroopers on a limited number of occasions. The AAC Captain recalled:

> In district compounds they had Joint Terminal Attack Controller (JTAC)(which were formerly Forward Air Controllers) and they would call us in. We used CIFS in one operation when the Paras were moving through an area flushing the [bad] guys out when they came up on [radio] net asking us to engage enemy in wood line – it did work. The enemy ran when we appeared. If they did not and were seen, they went to pieces – literally. The gun was our weapon of choice, it can be engaged quickly and accurately. You just kept your eyes on target. You only got a 10 to 15 second glimpse of the bad guys. If you chased them into a building then you put in a Hellfire and if they were hiding in a field you would use rockets.
>
> We did not use the Longbow radar to find targets, we used it to deconflict with other aircraft, to co-ordinate where everyone was coming in – Chinooks and jets. If we've scattered behind terrain after a contact then we could quickly work out where everyone was. Aircraft serviceability was very good. The forward looking infra-red [night sight] was epic – the clarity was good.

While the role of the AAC Apache squadrons in Afghanistan has received great prominence, the Lynx of 672 Squadron were also heavily involved in action during their year long tour from May 2006. Although the summer heat severely limited the performance and endurance of the Lynx, by moving to night operations in July and August 2006, 672 Squadron continued to make a contribution to the operation. As well as flying VIPs around Helmand province, the Lynx were also used heavily to fly escort or overwatch missions for British supply convoys, which were increasingly coming under Taliban attack.

Operation Herrick Lynx Squadron deployments to Afghanistan 2006–2010

Tour dates	Squadron	Aircraft type
May 06 to May 07	672 Sqn	Lynx AH.7
Oct 07 to Jan 08	659 Sqn	Lynx AH.7
Feb 08 to May 08	669 Sqn	Lynx AH.7
Nov 08 to Apr 09	847 Sqn	Lynx AH.7
Oct 09 to Jan 10	652 Sqn	Lynx AH.9
Feb 10 to May 10	651 Sqn	Lynx AH.9
May 10 to Jul 10	672 Sqn	Lynx AH.9A
Jul 10 to Nov 10	659 Sqn	Lynx AH.9A
Nov 10 to Feb 11	669 Sqn	Lynx AH.9A

The most daring Lynx operation occurred in August 2006 to recover a badly wounded Danish soldier from the besieged joint British-Danish base in Musa Qalah in northern Helmand province. The base's helicopter landing pad was being raked by Taliban fire on an hourly basis and it was considered too dangerous to fly a big and slow RAF Chinook into the base. So a 672 Squadron Lynx made a high speed dash into the base to get the wounded soldier before the Taliban could react. 'I will never forget that small helicopter suddenly dropping so fast out of the sky' recalled one Danish soldier who served in the besieged base. 'Several of us thought for a second that [the pilot] was going to pile in [his helicopter], he was a very good pilot and very brave. I salute him.' In a few minutes, the casualty was loaded safely on the Lynx and within the hour he was in the British hospital at Camp Bastion receiving treatment that saved his life

Perhaps the most famous Apache AH.1 combat mission to date occurred in January 2007 when a Royal Marines attack force tried to storm a Taliban base in a Jugroom Fort, near the town of Garmsir in southern Helmand, The Royal Marines were ambushed and had to withdraw. In the confusion, one Marine was left behind inside the fort. A Royal Artillery Lockheed Martin Desert Hawk mini-UAV located the body of the Marine inside the fort. Fearing the wounded or dead Marine would be seized by the Taliban, Royal Marine commanders wanted to launch an immediate rescue mission. The initial plan was hatched to use Viking vehicles for the rescue but they eventually concluded that the Apache attack helicopters would provide a quicker and safer means to get him out and back to safety.

The only helicopters on hand were a pair of AAC Apache AH.1s of 656 Squadron. Four Marines volunteered to strap themselves to the weapon pylons of the helicopters and fly into the fort to attempt a rescue. And so four British troops were strapped to the small side 'stub wings' of two Apaches, two to each helicopter. A third Apache provided aerial cover, and a further pair of Apache laid down a mass of covering fire while the first two Apache landed. All four men got off, as well as some of the aircrew, to provide additional firepower and to assist with the recovery of the missing Marine. The daring mission met little resistance and the Marines were able to load the body of their dead comrade on one of the helicopters to be flown back to safety.

Since May 2006, the main operational commitment of the AAC has been sustaining a squadron-sized detachment of eight operational Apache in Afghanistan. At first, with only two AAC squadrons qualified to fly the Apache a disproportionate burden fell on 9 Regiment in 2006 and 2007 to sustain the AH detachment in Afghanistan. After four months of intense combat over the summer of 2006, 656 Squadron handed over to 664 Squadron in August 2006. 656 Squadron returned to Afghanistan in December and eventually handed over the newly converted 664 Squadron in April.

Operation Herrick Attack Helicopter Squadron Deployments to Afghanistan, 2006–2010

Tour dates	Squadron
May to Aug 06	656 Sqn
Sept to Dec 06	664 Sqn
Jan to Apr 07	656 Sqn
May to Nov 07	662 Sqn
Dec 07 to Apr 08	663 Sqn
May to Aug 08	664 Sqn
Sept to Dec 08	654 Sqn
Jan to Apr 09	656 Sqn
May to Aug 09	662 Sqn
Sept to Dec 09	663 Sqn
Jan to Apr 10	653 Sqn
May to Aug 10	664 Sqn
Sept to Dec 10	654 Sqn

A forward detachment of Apache AH.1s operated from Camp Bastion during 2006 to provide a very high readiness alert capability. (AgustaWestland)

The AAC aimed to set up a two-year 'roulement' or formation cycle to allow each of its AH squadrons to spend four months at a time in theatre. Until 653 Squadron finished its conversion to the Apache in April 2009 this cycle could not be fully up and running. A two-year gap between Afghan deployments then became possible, which eased workload and reduced time away from home for AH Force personnel.

UK AH squadrons do not deploy with their own aircraft and equipment to Afghanistan but take over a pool or set of ten helicopters, ground support equipment, vehicles and spares based at Camp Bastion in the centre of Helmand province. These items were rotated home according to a maintenance and repair schedule that was not synchronized with unit handovers. 'When we go to Afghan we take over kit and vehicles already there, things stay in place' said an AAC Apache AH.1 pilot.

During deliberate operations it was also increasingly common for FARPs to be set up in UK forward operating bases (FOBs), such as FOBs Robinson, Dwyer and Edinburgh, on the outer fringes of Helmand provinces. 'More and more we are going to out stations,' said one AAC Afghan veteran. These deployments were often conducted by helicopter with ground crews, fuel and weapons moved by RAF Chinook to FOBs. When the UK helicopters were concentrated for a deliberate operation, considerable planning and preparation was involved over a forty-eight-hour period.

The British command in Helmand spent the later half of 2007 preparing the ground for major deliberate operations to win back the town of Musa Qalah that had been seized by the Taliban earlier in the year. A large air package of jet strike aircraft, USAF B-1B bombers, RAF Nimrod MR2 surveillance aircraft and USAF MQ-1 Predator unmanned aerial vehicles, co-ordinated by a USAF Boeing E-3C Sentry AWACS aircraft, was planned to support the assault on the town.

While columns of British and Afghan troops manoeuvred across the desert in the first week of December 2007 to surround the town, a battalion of US Paratroopers were flown to its outskirt to take the Taliban fighters by surprise in twelve US, UK and Dutch Chinooks. AAC Apache flew escort and fire support missions during the huge operation. The defenders initially put up strong resistance to the helicopter-landed troops and machine gun fire forced one of the supporting US Army Apache to make an emergency landing.

When the Taliban realized that the British and Afghans were poised to surround the town, their leaders ordered a retreat and soon the town was secured. Keeping the ground columns re-supplied soaked up a major portion of available UK and US helicopter resources. This operation also involved a significant portion of the NATO fixed-wing and UAV assets in southern Afghanistan. Its success was a major boost to morale of NATO and Afghan government forces.

The first eightheen months of the British campaign in Helmand province involved an unprecedented reliance on helicopters of the AAC and RAF.

Words such as 'critical', 'vital', 'essential', 'key', 'pivotal' and 'heroic' pepper Major General Gary Coward's description of the contribution that UK helicopters and their crews are making to the country's military operations in Afghanistan, Iraq and elsewhere.

General Coward the Commander, UK Joint Helicopter Command (JHC) during 2006 and 2007, commented at the time:

> In both theatres, deployed commanders are consistently asking for continued and enhanced helicopter support. In Iraq our role is lift and intelligence, surveillance, target acquisition and reconnaissance [ISTAR]. The deployed commander in Iraq sees helicopters as one of his key enablers, whereas in Afghanistan, because of the nature of the operation, terrain and the enemy, helicopters are a critical enabler.

He added that even ground convoys did not move around the south of the war-torn central Asian country without top cover from helicopters.

British troops rarely left their bases in Afghanistan during 2006 without top cover from heavily armed Apache AH.1s. (AgustaWestland)

The Afghanistan operation has given the JHC, which controls all battle-field helicopters of the AAC, RAF and Royal Navy, the chance to employ its Apache AH.1 attack helicopters in action for the first time and General Coward was enthusiastic about their performance.

> Apache is as good as I ever hoped for. We spent longer than planned developing the capability but, now it is deployed, I think it has shown its utility. It is a capability of first resort whenever our troops come into contact [with the enemy].

The Apache AH.1 stood up to the harsh Afghan environment better than many predictions, said General Coward, with the aircraft flying every day at a higher-than-expected rate.

> They have taken hits and survived. The Apache is as robust as they say on the tin. Every Apache flying hour I can afford is being flown in theatre. It is a capability in use in a whole variety of roles – overwatch, reconnaissance, ISTAR, show of force and escort. The only thing it does not do is lift kit and troops. The demand is there if we could provide more but there is also a need to husband it because we have not delivered the full force structure [of three attack helicopter regiments].

The intensity of operations by the Apache force can be gauged by the fact that 664 Squadron flew 2,147 hours during its August to November 2006 tour, firing 9,100 30mm rounds, 65 CRV-7 rockets and 28 AGM-114 Hellfire missiles.

The other UK helicopter type in Afghanistan, the AH.7, was also making a valuable contribution to operations and flying its allocated flight hours despite the effects of the summer heat and the high altitude on its performance, said General Coward.

General Coward was particularly impressed by reports from Afghanistan of the close integration of the Army Air Corps' AH.1 into ground operations by combat troops of 3 PARA, and lift operations by RAF Boeing Chinook HC.2 support helicopters. 'The level of close interoperability demonstrated by 656 Squadron's Apaches and the Chinooks of 18 and 27 Squadrons is a model that we should endeavour to export more widely in the command,' he said.

Praise for the high level of integration between land forces and helicopters was repeated by Brigadier Ed Butler, who said that '3 PARA would not go anywhere without attack helicopters because of the effect they had on the enemy. There is an unprecedented bond between 3 PARA and the helicopter crews' Other British officers described the level of cohesion between aircrew and ground troops as similar to that in UK's Special Forces helicopter wing.

The contribution of AAC and RAF helicopter crews to fighting in Helmand in 2006 and early 2007 has been rightly praised but with only eighteen helicopters – eight Apache, six Chinooks and four Lynx – deployed to Kandahar and Camp Bastion during this period, the number of helicopters in Afghanistan became a subject of great controversy. British helicopters and their crews saved the day on countless occasions but the UK military contingent just proved too small to achieve a decisive breakthrough against the Taliban. The war in Afghanistan would prove to be long and bloody.

Chapter 11

Army UAVs over Helmand

The bomb-making team could be clearly seen digging a hole in the wall of a compound to plant an improvised explosive device (IED) by cameras on a Hermes 450 unmanned aerial vehicle (UAV) operated by 32nd Regiment Royal Artillery. This was broad daylight and the insurgents were making no effort to hide their activities, relying on the proximity of civilians in nearby houses and compounds to protect them from NATO air attack. The challenge for the British Army UAV operators and intelligence analysts monitoring the event from Camp Bastion in central Helmand was to keep the insurgent bomb makers under surveillance long enough to glean actionable intelligence.

'We once followed an insurgent for fourteen hours and eventually lost him in a compound but this set us up to launch a search of the compound at a later date, ' a Hermes 450 operator recalled.

British Army UAV operations in Afghanistan benefited immensely from the experience in Iraq, although at first the UK troops did not have their own integral tactical UAV capability when they expanded their mission to Helmand Province in 2006.

The first British UAV deployment to the central Asian country occurred in October 2005 when 32nd Regiment's 18 Battery were tasked to conduct an operational trial of the latest variant of Desert Hawk I+ mini-UAV. The battery dispatched a team of twelve soldiers to Mazar-e-Sharif in northern Afghanistan and completed a very successful trial; the result of which paved the way for the purchase of more Desert Hawks and the committal of all of 18 Battery to Afghanistan in the spring of 2006 as part of 16 Air Assault Brigade.

The UAV detachments of the battery worked within the combat companies' 3rd Battalion, The Parachute Regiment, (3 PARA) to provide them with a real-time, day and night surveillance capability. Within days of deploying in May 2006, the battery's Desert Hawk I+ detachments were based in a handful of platoon house or district centres across Helmand Province, under

Hermes 450 unmanned aerial vehicles being prepared for missions over Helmand province at Camp Bastion in Afghanistan. (Thales)

A team of Taliban bombers is spotted by a Hermes 450 as they try to plant an improvised explosive devise intended to kill UK troops in Helmand province. (Thales)

remorseless attack by thousands of Taliban insurgents. The battery's deployment got off to an uncertain start, which reflected the British Army's unfamiliarity with the nature of the Taliban threat in Helmand province on 11 June when a Desert Hawk went astray on a mission outside a British base near the town of Sangin. A mission was ordered to recover the crashed UAV and the team was ambushed, leading in the subsequent confusion to the death of a Royal Artillery officer.

In October 2006, 18 Battery was replaced by colleagues from 42 Battery, which was to work with Royal Marines of 3 Commando Brigade. Perhaps the most famous Desert Hawk mission in Afghanistan occurred in January 2007 when a Royal Marines attack force tried to storm a Taliban base in a Jugroom Fort, near the town of Garmsir in southern Helmand, The Royal Marines were ambushed and had to withdraw. In the confusion, one Marine was left behind inside the fort. A 42 Battery Desert Hawk detachment was in the desert outside the town with the battlegroup headquarters as the battle

163

was unfolding. The detachment launched one of its UAVs to try to find the missing Royal Marine. After several minutes, an RAF imagery analyst and his 42 Battery colleagues had spotted the body of the young marine inside the fort and alerted senior commanders of the situation. The pictures were not clear enough to make out if the marine was dead or badly wounded.

Fearing he would be seized by the Taliban, Royal Marine commanders wanted to launch an immediate rescue mission. The initial plan was to use armoured vehicles for the rescue but they eventually concluded that the Apache attack helicopters would provide a quicker and safer means to get him out and back to safety. Four Marines volunteered to strap themselves to the weapon pylons of the helicopters and fly into the fort to attempt a rescue. Unfortunately, when the rescuers arrived the marine was found to be dead but the bravery of the rescuers achieved major prominence. It also showed that the Royal Marines of 3 Commando Brigade had embraced the potential of the Desert Hawk and 42 Battery was at the centre of its operations.

Imagery from Hermes 450s and other surveillance systems are analysed at 32nd Regiment Royal Artillery's 'ISTAR hub' at Camp Bastion.

The battery commander commented:

> As only the second Desert Hawk UAV battery to have deployed on Operation Herrick we are constantly facing new challenges both in operating a relatively immature capability as well as educating battlegroups to deploy Desert Hawk to best effect. Flight detachments face their own challenges; operating in support of isolated company locations, without re-supply for up to five weeks, with infrequent communications with Battery headquarters and in a harsh environment where mistakes are rarely forgiven. This requires highly competent and robust soldiers. For many of the members of the Battery this is a far cry from the duties they were carrying out as an air defence battery three years previous. The last three years has been a period of vast change for all Battery personnel. Re-equipping in eleven months from Rapier Field Standard C surface-to-air missiles in 22nd Regiment Royal Artillery to Phoenix in 32nd Regiment was particularly impressive. It required the whole battery to adopt a new career structure, train and then be deemed competent and current to fly Phoenix on operations in Iraq. Converting then from the Phoenix to the Desert Hawk posed yet more challenges and required a different skill set from operating the Phoenix from secure base locations to flying the Desert Hawk from the same trench as troops in contact. All achieved with the minimum of fuss and dedicated professionalism.

Since 32nd Regiment introduced the Hermes 450 into the Afghan and Iraqi theatres of operation in 2007 its organization and tactical employment has matured considerably. At first, 32nd Regiment was responsible for operating both the Hermes 450 and the newly acquired Lockheed Martin Desert Hawk III mini-unmanned aerial vehicle (MUAV) but the latter mission passed to the Royal Artillery's close air defence regiments.

57 Battery arrived in Afghanistan in the spring of 2007 and was soon the first unit in Afghanistan to operate the Hermes 450 UAV and it also continued to provide the Desert Hawk. The pressure to provide manpower for both types of UAVs in Iraq and Afghanistan, resulted in the decision being taken for the Royal Artillery's close air defence regiments to start taking over the mini-UAV mission. In October 2007, 18 Battery Command Group headed up the deployment of the Theatre UAV Battery (Afghanistan), which consisted of a Tactical UAV Troop from 18 Battery and Desert Hawk Detachments from 25/170 Battery of 47th Regiment. A similar-sized contingent from both batteries was simultaneously deployed to Iraq and this continued until the end of Operation Telic in mid-2009.

The arrival of the Hermes 450 dramatically transformed the British Army's UAV capability in Afghanistan, giving Task Force Helmand the ability for the first time to have its own true persistent ISTAR under its direct control. Several targets could now be placed under near continuous surveillance and imagery viewed by both senior commanders and staff in task force head-quarters at Lashkar Gah, as well as forward troops with access to remove viewing terminals, such as the L-3 Communications ROVER.

As commanders, at all levels, got more exposure to the Hermes 450 and the Desert Hawk, the British Army became more sophisticated in how it used them.

The Desert Hawk detachments were nearly always assigned to work with individual battlegroups in forward operating bases throughout Helmand bearing the brunt of responding to troops in contact (TIC) incidents.

The Hermes 450 became tasked almost exclusively for deliberate and pre-programmed ISTAR collection missions, although senior 32nd Regiment officers said there were occasions when there was always pull from senior commanders for it to be 'pulled towards TICs'.

The Hermes 450 is the largest UAV the Royal Artillery has ever operated and has to be treated like a manned aircraft in many respects. (Thales)

A senior 18 Battery officer during its deployment to Afghanistan in 2009–10 as part of the Operation Herrick 11 tour said both the Hermes 450 and Desert Hawk provided 'commanders with detailed, real-time images, by day and night, of what is going on behind their immediate line of sight'. He recalled:

> UAV operators are therefore very much the order of the day and as such the capability is in high demand. The Desert Hawk is routinely deployed in most forward operating and patrol bases. Indeed embedded as it is at battlegroup level it is quickly becoming a vital, 'must have' piece of equipment. The larger Hermes 450, meanwhile remains the principal intelligence and information gathering tool used at brigade level. As well as all its other capabilities, the system is currently at the centre of the provision of the positive identification of potential targets – a new legal requirement.

A tasking cycle was soon put in place that allowed a variety of organizations and agencies to request Hermes 450 support. These included the task force and battlegroup ISTAR staffs, Joint Airborne Reconnaissance Intelligence Centre (JARIC), signals intelligence staff and counter-IED operators. ISTAR staff in the task force headquarters collate requests for UAV support and then pass them to the theatre UAV battery operations room at Bastion, via their liaison officer in Lashkar Gah. The battery operations officer then tasks assets to collect the necessary intelligence. The collected product is

Contract personnel work around the clock at Camp Bastion to ensure Hermes 450s are available to fly missions over Helmand province. (Thales)

The Desert Hawk III mini-unmanned aerial vehicle is the primary system used to support front-line infantry battlegroups in Afghanistan. (Tim Ripley)

disseminated in variety of forms, including full motion video via remote viewing terminals, verbal reports over radio and satellite telephone, chat messages on the JChat system and formal written reports or target packs in Microsoft PowerPoint format emailed to customers.

32nd Regiment officers say one of the most important innovations has been the formation of what are termed ISTAR Tactical or Tac Parties. These are two-person teams that are highly mobile and routinely attached to infantry battlegroups around Helmand. As well as ISTAR expertise, they bring with them Hermes 450 remote viewing terminals, Harris 117 Tacsat radio and other communications links to the ISTAR Hub and allow infantry commanders to task Hermes UAVs to meet their needs and see the resulting product. L-3 Comm Rover 4 terminals are expected to be issued to the Tac Parties in the near future. 'Once they have ISTAR Tac Parties, the battle groups don't want to give them up,' say Royal Artillery officers.

> One of them was in the lead company assault during Operation Panther's Claw in July 2009. The key is that you need fit and robust people who understand ISTAR. ISTAR Tac Parties and Fire Support Teams [who control artillery, mortar and close air support] need to work closely together.

All elements of the Desert Hawk III can be broken down and man-packed by Royal Artillery soldiers accompanying infantry units. (Tim Ripley)

A single soldier launched the Desert Hawk III by simply throwing it into the air.
(Tim Ripley)

32nd Regiment is not formally established for sufficient ISTAR Tac Parties to meet the operational requirement and a senior 32nd Regiment officer said it had to move people around from other roles to set them up. At any one time there are six ISTAR Tac Parties in the UK's AO (area of operations) in Helmand. But this will be addressed in the future restructuring.

A female Royal Artillery who worked as the commander of an ISTAR Tac Party with 18 Battery in 2009–10 said they, 'worked directly with the ground commander, providing the downlink for any enabled UAV so as to allow him better situational awareness which, in turn, allowed more informed decision making.'

Her ISTAR Tac Party operated around Musa Qalah on a series of missions to drive the Taliban from positions in hills outside the town. She said:

> We set up an overwatch position to the north of the troops under-taking a operation. An American General Atomics MQ-9 Reaper was on station and identified a number of enemy firing points as our troops come in contact. The real success came when a Hermes 450 was tasked to track a suspected vehicle. As it did so we eventually discovered a whole insurgent re-supply chain, identify-ing a number of vehicles, buildings and mosques involved with weapon caches and re-supply. This is where the UAVs came into their own, not only supporting current operations as they happen, but helping with exploitation and planning future operations.

This incident also showed that the British Army was also becoming very adept at using multiple types of UAVs and other ISTAR systems to maximum effect in Afghanistan. On the complex and fast-moving Afghan battle-field, generating useable and timely information from the huge volumes of intelligence, surveillance, target acquisition and reconnaissance (ISTAR) sensor product available is an immense challenge. Inside its operations room in Camp Bastion, 32nd Regiment has set up what is known as the 'ISTAR Hub' to bring together all the major ISTAR units and systems operating in Helmand.

'Due to shortage of image analysts (IAs) in UK defence we developed the 'ISTAR Hub Concept' at Camp Bastion in November 2008,' said a 32nd Regiment officer.

> It is basically a pool of available IAs to the UK Task Force [in Afghanistan]. The benefit of the hub is that if the IAs did not sit next to each other in this way, they would not produce as much coherent product. By sticking two IAs together you trans-form the type of product and make it far more useful to the Task

Force commander. Camp Bastion became the hub because the theatre tactical UAV battery operations room had the feeds and we had the space.

The ISTAR Hub includes video feeds from the Hermes 450s that operate over Helmand on a daily basis, the ground station of the RAF's Raytheon Systems Airborne Stand-off Radar (ASTOR) Sentinel R1 aircraft, the post mission analysis section of the Royal Navy Westland Sea King Airborne Surveillance and Area Control (SKASAC) Mk 7 helicopters, the ground station from US and RAF operated MQ-9 Reapers, other US UAVs, down-links from fighter aircraft equipped with Rafael Litening and Lockheed Martin Sniper advanced targeting pods, post mission imagery tape analysis from AgustaWestland Apache AH.1 attack helicopters.

Working together the IAs from all the units co-located in the hub produce target packs that are distributed around the UK Task Force and coalition partners in Helmand. These can include long-term monitoring of specific geographical areas ahead of deliberate operations or dynamic tasking to locate and identify emerging targets such as specific insurgent leaders. The analysts also have access to the huge imagine reference library (IRL) that has been created by UK forces since operations started in southern Afghanistan in 2006.

According to 32nd Regiment officers, the ISTAR Hub has been a major step forward because it makes more efficient use of IAs and allows dynamic cross queuing of sensors. 'It allows the assimilation of corporate knowledge and enhances tactical understanding' said an officer. 'This allows the creation of fused multi-product target packs.'

British Army UAV operators call the hub a 'one stop shop for ISTAR products' but stress that the human interaction of all the players involved was the key to its success. They also emphasized that it allowed what he termed 'brigade (UK Task Force) ownership' of the ISTAR process that meant the collection and assets and IAs were focused on one single customer.

The hub was located in Camp Bastion, which is the main administrative base of UK forces in Helmand, rather than inside the UK Task Force Headquarters at Lashkar Gar in the provincial capital. It means that the senior command staff were not overloaded with raw imagery and data. A senior 32nd Regiment officer said:

At the start of this I was firmly of the view that the commander did not need to see the picture. The reality is that in a more complex environment an IA – who is usually a Lance Bombardier – in a Hermes 450 ground control station will regularly talk to the task force commander – a Brigadier. There is a place for live pictures in the HQ, but we need to avoid people developing a long screwdriver mentality.

Along with the rest of the British Army, 32nd Regiment has had to address how it can sustain an enduring commitment of a battery-sized unit to Afghanistan for the foreseeable future.

In 2009 it was able to stand-up an extra battery of 100 or so soldiers bringing the unit up to an establishment of 750 people to allow the regiment to establish a formation readiness cycle, so soldiers will spend six months in Afghanistan and then have a two-year break at home before returning to Helmand.

This means that at any one time a battery will be in Afghanistan, another will be preparing to deploy, one will be starting pre-deployment training and the other two will be doing training support or preparing for other contingent operations.

Royal Artillery officers plan a Hermes 450 mission during a training exercise in the UK. (Tim Ripley)

The newly formed 43 (Lloyd's Company) Battery undertook conversion to role training and was ready for operations in October 2010.

A senior 32nd Regiment officer said:

At first we flew mini and tactical UAVs in both theatres and had a 12-month tour interval but this was unsustainable. At any one time we always have people deployed. The only way the commanding officer can get all six Battery Commanders in a conference room together is to pull one in from his mid tour R&R. But we have now got video conferencing to hold meetings with our team in theatre.

Royal Artillery UAV Battery Deployments to Afghanistan, 2005 to 2011 – Operation Herrick

Tour Date	Battery	Equipment
May to Oct 06	18 (Quebec 1759) Battery	Desert Hawk I+
Nov 06 to Apr 07	42 (Alem Hamza) Battery	Desert Hawk I+
May 07 to Nov 07	57 (Bhurtpore 1825–1826) Battery	Hermes 450 & Desert Hawk III
Nov 07 to Apr 08	18 (Quebec 1759) Battery	Hermes 450
Nov 07 to Apr 08	21 (Air Assault) Battery	Desert Hawk III
Apr to Oct 08	42 (Alem Hamza) Battery	Hermes 450
Apr to Oct 08	25/170 (Imjin) Battery	Desert Hawk III
Oct 08 to Apr 09	57 (Bhurtpore 1825-1826) Battery	Hermes 450
Oct 08 to Apr 09	10 (Assaye) Battery	Desert Hawk III
Apr to Oct 09	22 (Gibraltar 1779–1783) Battery	Hermes 450
Apr to Oct 09	9 (Plassey) Battery	Desert Hawk III
Nov 09 to May 10	18 (Quebec 1759) Battery	Hermes 450
Nov 09 to May 10	58 (Eyres) Battery	Desert Hawk III
May 10 to Nov 10	42 (Alem Hamza) Battery	Hermes 450
May 10 to Nov 10	12 (Minden) Battery	Desert Hawk III
Nov 10 to Apr 11	57 (Bhurtpore 1825-1826) Battery	Hermes 450
Nov 10 to Apr 11	21 (Air Assault) Battery	Desert Hawk III

32nd Regiment is continuing to evolve the training its personnel receive before heading to Afghanistan. This is carried out both in the UK, overseas and in theatre because of the unusual procurement method used to acquire the Hermes 450 under the UK's urgent operational requirement (UOR) process.

The regiment's UAV operators – mission commanders, payload operators, pilots – now follow a structured training regime that begins with a six-week generic tactical UAV course at the Royal School of Artillery at Larkhill. This is followed by fifteen days of theory and five days of simulator training in UK before crews complete three weeks' live flying training on the Hermes

450. Two weeks' theory and combined tactical training on the Hermes 450 then have to be completed in the UK.

Competency, concurrency and external validation to fly in theatre is carried out in Afghanistan before operators gain their theatre qualification and are allowed to fly the Hermes without supervision.

This combined tactical training element has recently been enhanced with the running of a final exercise combining simulator training and tactical procedures for UAV tasking, mission planning and processing intelligence product.

'It is the culmination of technical training' a 32nd Regiment battery commander said. 'The theatre qualification delivers a melding of technical with tactical skills.'

18 Battery's exercise, named Quebec Finale, was carried out in September 2009 in a building designed to simulate the theatre battery's operations room in Camp Bastion. Student crews enter the building and have to sign for their aircraft from Royal Electrical Mechanical Engineer (REME) representatives as they would in theatre. They then have to pick up airspace management information and tactical information to allow them to plan their mission. After going out to a simulator in the grounds of Robert's Barracks, the crews

The Hermes 450 is expected to serve in Afghanistan at least until the end of 2011 when the Watchkeeper will take over from it. (Thales)

fly their training mission and talk over simulated radio nets to instructors 'playing' other agencies. At the same time, intelligence analysts are downloading imagery from the simulator and creating targeting packs on computer work stations in the 'simulated' ISTAR Hub.

All through this process, instructors who have recently served in Helmand are on hand to mentor students through the tactical situation. An officer in 57 Battery said:

> I was operations officer on Operation Herrick 9 with 3 Commando Brigade. I am mentoring the operations officer who is going to Operation Herrick 12 in a few weeks' time.

In August 2009, UK Prime Minister Gordon Brown announced that Hermes 450 operations in Afghanistan were being stepped up to counter the Taliban IED threat. This was to see 32nd Regiment add an extra tasking line or daily Hermes 450 mission to its operations, above its then average of 19 sorties over some 205 flight hours a month. In more than two years of operations in Afghanistan the regiment had amassed over 30,000 flight hours by late 2010, with 18 Battery alone flying nearly 9,000 hours in just over 4,500 sorties in the six months up to May 2010.

A senior 32nd Regiment officer said the British Army's 12 Desert Hawk detachment's flew 2,394 hours and made 3954 flights during 18 Battery's tour. The Desert Hawk was described as 'agile and responsive' by one of the batteries officers, who said British troops in forward operating bases (FOBs), were 'clamouring for it'. 'They own it, decide when to fly it and where it will fly,' he said. 'They put it up when patrols go out of FOBs.'

32nd Regiment's Hermes 450 battery at Camp Battery made 570 flights and flew 6,555 hours during 18 Battery's tour bring the types total flight hours in Afghanistan to 30,000 hours since 2007. The Hermes 450 were airborne for up to 14 hours each day. The dissemination of Hermes 450 full-motion video imagery was also soon be expanded by setting up a network of microwave towers by the British Army, known as the Helmand Triangle, that will link Camp Bastion and other British bases. The performance of the Hermes 450 air vehicles was also being improved by the introduction of the DGPS automatic take-off and landing system during late 2010.

With the Afghan war still raging, the services of the British Army's UAVs will be in demand for many years to come.

Chapter 12

Army Air in 2012

British Army air operations are conducted by regiments, squadrons and independent sub-units of the Army Air Corps (AAC) and Royal Artillery. The two organizations have very separate peacetime chains of command but on operational deployments it is common for the British Army to group them under a single commander, who may be responsible for all combat intelligence, surveillance, target acquisition and reconnaissance (ISTAR) or offensive strike missions in a specific theatre or area of responsibility.

Army Air Corps

It was not until 1978 when the TOW missile-armed Westland Lynx AH.1 armed helicopters entered service that the AAC became a fully fledged combat arm of the British Army. The AAC is one of the British Army's three combat arms, which along with the Special Forces have the mission of engaging in direct contact with the enemy.

Manned army helicopters and aircraft are employed in five roles on the battlefield. These are:

- Offensive action or the application of firepower and manoeuvre in order to defeat the enemy.
- ISTAR – the use of army aviation to gather information using optical and electronic devices.
- Control and direction of firepower – this involves observing enemy forces and their engagement with other weapon systems such as close air support by fast jets, main battle tanks, artillery and mortars, land-based rocket systems or even naval gunfire support.
- Command support – providing the capability for commanders to move around quickly on the battle field.
- Movement of personnel and materiel – the support to specialist operations, helicopter medical evacuation and delivery of vital equipment.

Although the AAC has been an established part of the British Army's order of battle since 1957, over the past decade the control of rotary wing aircraft in the UK armed forces has undergone considerable transformation. Control of battlefield helicopters and aircrew training is now the responsibility of tri-service headquarters dubbed the Joint Helicopter Command (JHC) so the Director of the Army Aviation (DAAvn) no longer has 'end-to-end' control of army flying.

DAAvn is often called the 'tribal chief' of the AAC and he runs the Head-quarters AAC at Middle Wallop. His main role is to act as the single point of advice on army aviation (except unmanned aerial vehicles) for the Chief of the General Staff and other senior army commanders. DAAvn, however, has responsibility for the airworthiness of army UAVs and is involved in assessing the safety rules for their flight operations. Middle Wallop is home to the recently re-branded Army Aviation Centre. This is host to the Army Aviation Centre, which is responsible for initial AAC aircrew selection and subsequently conversion to type (CTT), as well as advanced training of AAC badged ground crew. This training activity is formally under the control of the British Army's Director General of Recruiting and Training. The main element of the AAC's aircrew pipeline is controlled on behalf of Headquarters JHC by tri-service Defence Helicopters Flying School (DHFS) and industry-run Military Flying Training Service (MFTS). AAC helicopters pilots undergo their basic flying training at the DHFS at RAF Shawbury in Shropshire. Fixed-wing aircrew trained in 2010 under a commercial contract at Oxford Air Training Services because in 2009–10 the MFTS did not have enough capacity on its Beechcraft King Air aircraft at RAF Cranwell in Lincolnshire.

In the UK, operational AAC units are controlled by the tri-service Joint Helicopter Command, which is based within the British Army's Headquarters Army Command at Marlborough Lines, Andover, in Hampshire. The JHC is responsible for generating units and personnel that are fit to deploy on overseas operations under the direction of the Permanent Joint Head-quarters (PJHQ) at Northwood in west London. Once deployed in theatre, control of AAC units usually passes to a JHC forward headquarters. In the case of the current war in Afghanistan, this is designated JHF (Afghanistan) (JHF (A)) and it is commanded in rotation by AAC, Royal Navy and RAF officers, supported by staff from the British Army, Royal Navy and RAF.

JHF(A) has day-to-day operational control of all UK helicopters in Afghanistan but it is under the direct command of the NATO Regional Command (South-West) Headquarters at Camp Bastion. UK helicopters operate across southern Afghanistan in support of NATO forces and it also means the UK-led Task Force Helmand can call upon coalition helicopters in a crisis. Once helicopters receive their daily tasking, they are often placed under the direct tactical control of ground forces battlegroups or joint terminal attack controllers (JTAC) for specific operations.

JHC is also responsible for providing helicopters and personnel to support civil emergency services and law enforcement agencies in the UK. Outside of JHC, several commercially-operated and military-registered (COMR) helicopters based in the UK, Belize and Brunei, which are controlled by Headquarters Land Forces for training support tasks. The future of the Belize detachment is in doubt after the October 2010 Strategic Defence Review (SDSR) recommended the run down of British Army jungle training in the Central American country. It seems likely the helicopters will be transferred to Kenya to support the growing training mission there, which prepares units for deployments to Afghanistan.

The procurement of helicopters and provision of logistic support to the AAC is the responsibility of the Defence Equipment & Support (DE&S) organization at Abbey Wood in Bristol. It has specific teams, formerly known as 'integrated project teams' (IPTs), that manage individual helicopter programmes. The Apache Team is the largest one supporting the AAC and it manages the Apache Integrated Operational Support (AIOS) contract in co-operation with AgustaWestland, Boeing, Lockheed Martin and other sub-contractors. The Lynx, Puma and Gazelle, Helicopters/Islander, and Helicopter Engine Teams support other AAC aircraft and helicopter types, organizing maintenance, purchasing spares and dealing with contractors. The latter role is particularly important where COMR helicopters are concerned.

The AAC's 67 Apache AH.1s are at the heart of all its activities. (Tim Ripley)

Army Air Corps Order of Battle, 2011

Unit	Base	Type	Role
UK BASED UNITS			
660 Squadron RAF	Shawbury, Shropshire	Eurocopter Squirrel HT.1	Basic rotary-wing training
674 Squadron	RAF Barkston Heath, Lincolnshire Middle Wallop, Hampshire	Slingsby T.67M Firefly 260	Primary training
HQ Army Air Corps Centre	Middle Wallop, Hampshire		
667 Squadron		Westland Lynx AH.7, Westland Gazelle AH.1, AgustaWestland Apache AH.1	Development & trials
Army Historic Aircraft Flight		Auster AOP.9, DHC 1 Chipmunk T.10, de Havilland Beaver AL.1, Sud Alouette AH.2, Westland Scout AH.1, Bell Sioux AH.1, Saunders-Roe Skeeter AOP.12	Display flying
School of Army Aviation 2 & 7 Regiment	Middle Wallop, Hampshire		
670 Squadron		Eurocopter Squirrel HT.2	Advanced rotary-wing training
671 Squadron		Westland Lynx AH.7, Westland Gazelle AH.1, Bell 212HP AH.1	Operational training
673 Squadron		AgustaWestland Apache AH.1	Operational training
AH Force Headquarters	Wattisham, Suffolk		
3 Regiment	Wattisham, Suffolk		
653 Squadron		AgustaWestland Apache AH.1	Attack
662 Squadron		AgustaWestland Apache AH.1	Attack
663 Squadron		AgustaWestland Apache AH.1	Attack
4 Regiment	Wattisham, Suffolk		
654 Squadron		AgustaWestland Apache AH.1	Attack
656 Squadron/AMTAT		AgustaWestland Apache AH.1	Attack
664 Squadron		AgustaWestland Apache AH.1	Attack
5 Regiment	Aldergrove, Northern Ireland		
665 Squadron		Westland Gazelle AH.1	Observation
651 Squadron		Britten-Norman Defender 4S AL.1	Utility/ liaison/ observation

Unit	Base	Type	Role
6 Regiment (V) (TA)	Bury St Edmonds		
655 (Scottish Horse) Squadron	Middle Wallop, Hampshire		FARP Teams
677 (Suffolk Yeomanry & Norfolk Yeomanry)	Bury St Edmonds		FARP Teams
9 Regiment	Dishforth, North Yorkshire		
659 Squadron		Westland Lynx AH.7/9A	Light utility
669 Squadron		Westland Lynx AH.7/9A	Light utility
672 Squadron		Westland Lynx AH.7/9A	Light utility
Joint Special Forces Aviation Wing			
657 Squadron	Odiham, Hampshire	Westland Lynx AH.7/9A SF	Support
8 Flight	Credenhill, Herefordshire	AS365N3 SF	Support
GERMANY			
1 Regiment	Gutersloh, Germany		
652 Squadron		Westland Lynx AH.7/9A	Light utility
661 Squadron		Westland Lynx AH.7/9A	Light utility
OTHER OVERSEAS BASED UNITS			
7 Flight	Seria, Brunei	Bell 212HP AH.1	Support
25 Flight****	Belize City, Belize	Bell 212HP AH.1	Support
29 (BATUS) Flight	Suffield, Canada	Westland Gazelle AH.1	Support

Notes:
**   Regiment to transfer to UK
***   674 Squadron is part of No. 1 Elementary Flying Training School at RAF Barkston Heath (with a Middle Wallop detachment).
**** To close in 2011?

Key:
AHTU	Advanced Helicopter Training Unit
AMTAT	Air Manoeuvre Training and Advisory Unit
BATUS	British Army Training Unit Suffield
TA	Territorial Army

The core of the AAC is its five flying regiments, which provide the force elements to JHC and PJHQ. In early 2011 AAC manpower totalled around 2,140. Unlike the Royal Navy and RAF, almost two-thirds of AAC pilots are non-commissioned officers. Some 2,000 support personnel from the Royal Electrical Mechanical Engineers (REME), Royal Logistic Corps (RLC) and other specialists units are assigned to work within AAC regiments and squadrons. The AAC force structure comprises just under 4,000 personnel.

Joint operations between Apache AH.1s and Lynx AH.9As are paving the way for the introduction of the Lynx Wildcat in 2014. (Tim Ripley)

At the cutting edge of current AAC operations are the two attack helicopter (AH) units, 3 and 4 Regiments, which comprise the Attack Helicopter Force at Wattisham Flying Station in Suffolk. The AH Force is almost totally committed to operations in Afghanistan and has been significantly re-organized to ensure that between eight and 10 AgustaWestland Apache AH.1s with supporting air and ground crews can be sustained in Helmand Province for the foreseeable future.

When the Apache was originally purchased in 1996 it was envisaged that it would operate in mixed regiments with Westland Lynx AH.7/9s acting as a light utility and scout helicopter. This concept has now been dropped and the AH regiments are purely equipped with the Apache.

Each regiment takes turns to be responsible for providing personnel in Afghanistan for a twelve-month period. Within that period, each of the regiment's three squadrons does a four-month tour in Afghanistan and regimental headquarters personnel serve in the JHF(A) organization throughout the year.

All the Apache airframes are held centrally in a pool and allocated to specific tasks. Under the AIOS contract AgustaWestland is responsible for generating airframes on a daily basis. Currently the company has to provide twenty-two to the UK-based regiment at Wattisham, between four and six are permanently based in Arizona for Crimson Eagle and ten are in Afghanistan. A further twelve Apache are based at Middle Wallop for CTT training and trials. At any one time ten to twelve helicopters are undergoing scheduled major servicing at the AgustaWestland-run Depth Support Unit at Wattisham and five are held in storage at Wattisham as attrition reserves.

The next most important helicopter types in AAC service are the Lynx AH.7 and AH.9, which are operated by 1 Regiment at Gütersloh in Germany and 9 Regiment at Dishforth in North Yorkshire. The former has two squadrons and the latter has three squadrons. These units are now fully committed to a rota providing a squadron's worth of personnel in Afghanistan who operate five Lynx AH.9As in the light utility (LUH) and manned aerial surveillance (MAS) roles. As with the AH Force, the Lynx helicopters are held in a pool and allocated according to task. All Lynx helicopters undergo depth maintenance at Vector Aerospace's facility at Fleetlands in Hampshire.

JHC Flying Station Aldergrove in Northern Ireland is the home of 5 Regiment, which during the height of 'the Troubles' in 1980s and 1990s bore the brunt of support for army operations against the Provisional IRA. This is very much in the past and the regiment's two squadrons are now dedicated to global operations. 651 Squadron is the AAC centre of excellence for MAS and operates a mixed fleet of Britten-Norman Islander AL.1 and Defender 4 Al.1 twin-engined aircraft. These aircraft have seen extensive service in Iraq, Afghanistan and Northern Ireland. After the disbandment

Realistic live firing training is an essential requirement during pre-deployment training for Afghanistan. (AgustaWestland)

AAC pilots are only deployed on operations in Afghanistan after intensive training lasting several months. (Tim Ripley)

of 7 (Volunteers) Regiment and 12 Flight in Germany on 1 April 2009, 5 Regiment's 665 Squadron is the last AAC squadron-sized unit to operate the veteran Westland Gazelle AH.1.

In October 2009 it was announced by Defence Equipment & Support Minister Quentin Davies MP, that the Gazelle out-of-service date was being extended to 2018. It had been thought that the demise of the Gazelle in 2012 would likely see the disbandment of 5 Regiment or its conversion into a purely fixed-wing unit and possibly its return to the UK mainland. Apparently 665 Squadron's Gazelles had been reprieved and it seemed that 5 Regiment would continue to operate in its existing form for most of the next decade. This, however, appears to have been overturned in the October 2010 SDSR, which recommended the early retirement of the Gazelle. It seems, however, that the five Gazelles serving with 29 Flight in Canada will be replaced by COMR aircraft to reduce costs and enhance their casualty evacuation capability.

Defensive aid systems are now fitted to all AAC helicopters that are deployed on operations in Afghanistan. (Tim Ripley)

The AAC's Territorial Army (TA) or reserve component has undergone major changes over the past five years with the disbandment of its last flying unit 7 (Volunteers) Regiment earlier this year. But the establishment of 6 (Volunteers) Regiment has boosted the involvement of the TA in Apache and Lynx operations. This unit provides individual personnel to work at forward arming and refuelling points (FARP), Lynx door gunners and aircrew. The regiment initially only had one squadron but a second stood up in 2010.

Royal Artillery UAVs

The British Army's unmanned aerial vehicle (UAV) force is currently operated almost exclusively by the Royal Artillery. Over the past decade elements of four Royal Artillery regiments have operated a variety of UAVs but by 2010, UAV operations had be concentrated in two Regular and one Territorial Army regiments. This constantly evolving structure reflects the pace of UAV developments and the rapid acquisition of new systems by the Royal Artillery over the past decade.

Even at the start of 2011 this pace of change seems unlikely to reduce as the Royal Artillery prepared to accept the first Thales Watchkeeper 450 system into service and then deploy it into Afghanistan.

Few major British Army exercises now do not feature participation by AAC Apache AH.1 detachments. (Tim Ripley)

The core of Royal Artillery UAV expertise has resided in 32nd Regiment for most of the decade and the unit has taken almost every new UAV system into service during that period. The main exception to this was in April 2010, when the Royal Engineers introduced the fourth main type of UAV type in UK service. The Honeywell Tarantula Hawk vertical take-off and landing mini UAV is launched from Mastiff mine-protected vehicles without the operator having to leave the cover of the vehicle. In 2011 control of the Tarantula Hawk will migrate from the Royal Engineers to the Royal Artillery to ensure the flight safety reporting chain is effective.

At the start of 2010, 32nd Regiment comprised five operational batteries that were all trained to operate the Hermes 450 system. Its batteries are all participating in a scheduled rotation of UAV personnel to Afghanistan to operate the Hermes 450s. The fifth sub-unit, 43 Battery, was formed in 2009 to ease the pressure of Afghanistan rotations and allow soldiers to spend

Some thirty years after entering service, the Lynx AH.7 is near the end of its time on front-line duty and has been replaced in Afghanistan by the Lynx AH.9A. (Tim Ripley)

The Lynx AH.9A is proving a major success in Afghanistan thanks to its new uprated engines. (Tim Ripley)

more time at home between operational deployments. Each battery comprises around 100 soldiers and the 32nd Regiment's total strength was some 750 personnel.

The regiment's personnel fly and command the UAVs on operational missions, while civilian contractors provided by UAV Tactical Systems Ltd (U-TacS) repair the air vehicles, as well as launching and recovering them from the runway at Camp Bastion. These contractors are all UK and US citizens and achieved notoriety when a British tabloid newspaper discovered that one was a remote-controlled model aircraft enthusiast. The use of contractors also meant that 32nd Regiment's personnel could concentrate on mission specific tasks related to flying the air vehicle and operating its sensors.

32nd Regiment is scheduled to receive the first Watchkeeper 450 UAVs during 2011 and it is increasingly involved in test and evaluation activity, as well as running training courses on the new system. A suite of Watchkeeper simulators was installed at Robert's Barracks in 2010.

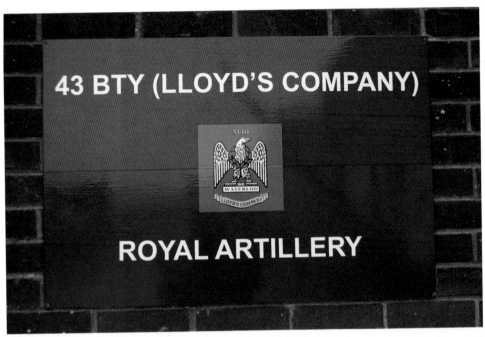

Robert's Barracks at Larkhill on Salisbury Plain is home to 32nd Regiment Royal Artillery and up until the end of 2011 43 (Lloyd's Company) Battery. (Tim Ripley)

Since 2007, the Royal Artillery's two close air defence regiments, 12th and 47th Regiment, have been taking turns to provide troops to operate the Desert Hawk III in Iraq and Afghanistan. This relieved the pressure on 32nd Regiment, which concentrated on operating the Hermes 450. As a result, between 2007 and 2009 at any one time half a battery from 32nd Regiment to operate the big tactical UAV and half a battery from one of the close air defence regiments to operate Lockheed Martin Desert Hawk III mini-UAVs (MUAVs) were deployed in Iraq. When the Iraq commitment concluded in May 2009, UAV operations ramped up in Afghanistan and a full battery from 32nd Regiment and from the air defence regiment would be deployed at any one time. By mid-2010 this involved sustaining three continuous orbits or task lines of Hermes 450s and eleven MUAV detachments. Each MUAV detachment was a five-strong self-contained team of personnel ready to operate with infantry battlegroups at forward operating bases.

In May 2010 the British Army announced the formation of its second UAV regiment to better sustain its operation of mini UAVs in Afghanistan, by formally re-roling 47th Regiment Royal Artillery. This was part of the British Army's Operation Entirety effort to optimize its structure and training to sustain its presence in Afghanistan. Under the plans it is proposed that both regiments will have personnel capable of operating both the Hermes 450 and Desert Hawk III.

By establishing 47th Regiment as a dedicated UAV unit it is hoped that training and logistic support will be improved on a long-term basis, as well as easing rotation issues. It is now intended that both 32nd and 47th Regiments will have batteries operating the Watchkeeper system when it enters service.

12th Regiment will now concentrate on training and operating the Thales High Velocity Missile (HVM) as part of 1 (UK) Armoured Division, making it the sole close air defence unit of the British Army. Under the reorganization, 47th Regiment moved from the control of 3 (UK) Division to 1 Artillery Brigade, alongside 32nd Regiment, as part of the Theatre Troops organization, which oversees the Army's specialist units.

104th Regiment Royal Artillery (Volunteers) is the Territorial Army's only UAV regiment. Its part-time soldier regularly deploy as individuals or small groups to Afghanistan to augment the batteries of their Regular Army counterparts, in 32nd and 47th Regiments, where they operate both mini and

The Hermes 450 has transformed the British Army's unmanned aerial vehicle capability. (Thales)

Desert Hawk III mini-unmanned aerial vehicles are used widely to support infantry battlegroups in Afghanistan. (Tim Ripley)

tactical air vehicles in support of ground operations in Helmand province. Soldiers from the regiment have also served in Iraq and in June 2011 thirty-five members of the regiment deployed for six months on United Nations operations in Cyprus.

Continuing financial pressures on the UK defence budget during 2011 forced the British Army to look again at its organisation and it was decided that 32nd and 47th Regiments were to be re-organised around five so-called 'mirror batteries' configured to operate both mini and tactical UAVs.

Royal Artillery UAV-equipped Regiments, 2012

32nd Regiment Royal Artillery
Robert's Barracks, Larkhill, Wiltshire
22 (Gibraltar 1779–1783) Battery
18 (Quebec 1759) Battery
42 (Alem Hamza) Battery (to disband late 2011)

Unmanned aerial vehicles are now embedded in all aspects of British Army operations in Afghanistan. Here a Hermes 450 lands at Camp Bastion. (Thales)

43 (Lloyd's Company) Battery (to disband late 2011)
57 (Bhurtpore 1825–1826) Battery
46 (Talavera) Battery (headquarters and supply element)
Workshops Royal Electrical Mechanical Engineers (REME) (repair element)

47th Regiment Royal Artillery
Baker Barracks, Thorney Island, Hampshire
10 (Assaye) Battery
21 (Air Assault) Battery
25/170 (Imjin) Battery (to disband late 2011)
31 (Headquarter) Battery (headquarters and supply element)
Workshops Royal Electrical Mechanical Engineers (REME) (repair element)

104 Regiment Royal Artillery (Volunteers)
211 (South Wales) Battery
Cardiff and Abertillery
214 (Worcestershire) Battery
Dancox House, Worcester
217 (City of Newport) Battery
Raglan Barracks, Newport

Chapter 13

AH Force

The UK announced it would buy the Apache in July 1995 and signed the main £2.9 billion procurement contract nine months later with the then Westland Helicopters. This saw the Yeovil-based company assembling the majority of the helicopters in the UK and helping McDonnell Douglas (now Boeing) integrate UK specific Rolls-Royce Turbomeca RTM-322 engines, weapons and the GEC-Marconi (now BAE Systems) Helicopter Integrated Defensive Aids Suite (HIDAS) and Bristol Aerospace CRV-7 free-flight rockets.

The first nine Yeovil-assembled Apache were handed over to the AAC in January 2001 but it would be five years before the acceptance or military aircraft release process would be complete. The biggest hurdle faced by the AAC AH Force was training enough air and ground crew fast enough to build up the force structure at the required pace. Technical problems with the aircrew flight simulators played havoc with the fielding plan and this went through a number of evolutions until 2003 when the first conversion-to-type training course eventually got underway at the School of Army Aviation at Middle Wallop. The following year 656 Squadron completed conversion-to-role training and was declared combat ready in October 2004. In the spring of 2005, the first attachment helicopter regiment, 9 Regiment AAC, was declared combat ready after its second sub-unit, 664 Squadron, completed conversion-to-role training.

At this point, the British Army was still envisaging fielding its Apache in mixed regiments with two squadrons of eight attack helicopters and one of eight Westland Lynx AH.7 light utility/observation helicopters. First to get the Apache would be 9 Regiment at Dishforth Airfield in North Yorkshire and then 3 and 4 Regiments at Wattisham Flying Station in Suffolk would be equipped with the attack helicopters. Events in Afghanistan would soon conspire to throw the AAC's plans into flux again and by the autumn of 2006, the Apache fielding plan would be changed once again.

The Apache AH.1 provides the AAC and the British Army with awesome airborne firepower. (Tim Ripley)

The deployment of 16 Air Assault Brigade to Afghanistan in the spring of 2006 saw the UK Apache Force get its combat debut. Crews of 656 Squadron fired their first Lockheed Martin AGM-114 Hellfire missiles in anger on 20 May 2006 when they destroyed a French army jeep that had been captured by Taliban insurgents near Kajaki. The rest, as they say, is history.

Thousands of insurgents swarmed across the war-torn province besieging British Paratroopers for weeks at a time in a series of remote outposts across Helmand province, known as Platoon Houses. They came to rely on helicopters to bring in supplies and evacuate the wounded. The eight Apache in Afghanistan were flying around 400 hours a month in July and August, rather than the 180 hours a month that had been programmed for the whole of the UK Apache Force during 2006.

The seriousness of the situation in Afghanistan was starting to sink in back in the higher echelons of the AAC, the tri-service Joint Helicopter Command which had day-to-day control of the AH Force and the Defence

Logistic Organizations (DLO) (now Defence Equipment & Support DE&S organization). Preparations had to be rapidly made to generate the required number of aircrew, ground crews and weapons for Afghanistan for several years to come.

The AAC also needed to re-organize the AH Force to speed up the training of aircrew and ground crew. In the summer of 2006 only two Apache squadrons were combat ready and by the end of 2007 only four squadrons would be fit to go to war. This put at risk the ability to continuously rotate personnel through the war zone and not 'burn them out'.

The first move to turn this around took place in July 2006 when the Ministry of Defence announced that the AH Force would be concentrated at Wattisham between June and September 2007. The two Apache squadrons at Dishforth, 656 and 664 Squadrons, would be transferred to 4 Regiment, turning 9 Regiment into a pure Lynx unit. While 3 and 4 Regiment would each eventually boast three Apache squadrons.

These two regiments became the core of the AH Force at Wattisham Flying Station in Suffolk. Each regiment took turns to be responsible for providing personnel in Afghanistan for a twelve-month period. Within that period, each of the regiment's three squadrons now does a four-month tour in

Apache AH.1s of 664 Squadron AAC prepare for a training mission over Northumberland in August 2009. (Tim Ripley)

The AAC's Attack Helicopter Force is sustained by an industry partnership of AgustaWestland, Boeing, Lockheed Martin and the UK's Defence Equipment & Support organization. (Tim Ripley)

Afghanistan and regimental headquarters personnel serve in the Joint Helicopter Force (Afghanistan) organization throughout the year.

The regiment that is not in Afghanistan, has responsibility for flying operations at Wattisham and supporting a range of training activities around the world. The most important of these is pre-deployment training (PDT) for AH Force personnel heading to Afghanistan, which culminates in the twice yearly Exercise Crimson Eagle in Arizona and California, and results in Apache aircrew being declared combat ready. A major part of these efforts is the maintenance of an effective training pipeline of Apache aircrew, through the running of conversion to role (CTR) courses by the Air Manoeuvre Training and Advisory Team (AMTAT).

Almost every major UK exercise run by the British Army, as well as many Royal Marines and Royal Air Force exercises, now involves some sort of AH participation. The majority of these are pre-deployment or mission rehearsal exercises (MRX) for units heading to Afghanistan.

All the AAC Apache airframes are held centrally in a pool and allocated to specific tasks. Under the October 2009 Apache Integrated Operational Support (AIOS) contract, AgustaWestland is responsible for generating airframes on a daily basis. Currently, the company has to provide twenty-two

197

The heart of the AAC Attack Helicopter Force is its highly trained aircrew. (Tim Ripley)

airframes to the UK-based regiment at Wattisham, six are permanently based in the US for the Crimson Eagle twice yearly live firing exercise and ten are in Afghanistan. A further twelve Apache are based at Middle Wallop for conversion-to-type training and trials. At any one time ten to twelve helicopters are undergoing scheduled major servicing at the AgustaWestland-run Depth Support Unit (DSU) at Wattisham and five are held in climate controlled storage at the Suffolk base as attrition reserves.

The home-based regiment is tasked with running all the flying activities at Wattisham, including managing a common pool of aircraft, running the airfield's flight line and carrying out minor servicing. From April 2008, Wattisham has had an RAF-style station commander or force commander to better manage resources at the base.

By the middle of 2009 the AAC had set up a two-year 'roulement' or formation cycle to allow each of its AH squadrons to spend four months at a time in theatre. Until the last AH sub-unit, 653 Squadron, finished its conversion to the Apache in April, this cycle could not be fully up and

Preparing for action. An Apache AH.1 crew from 664 Squadron pre-flight their aircraft. (Tim Ripley)

The AAC is well on the way to retro-fitting all its Apache AH.1s with the more capable MTADS night vision system. (Tim Ripley)

running. Many of personnel from 9 and 3 Regiment in 2006 and 2007 were spending two four-month long tours a year in Afghanistan because the full force of six squadrons had not been fully fielded. A two-year gap between Afghan deployments is now possible, which eases workload and reduces time away from home for AH Force personnel.

UK AH squadrons do not deploy with their own aircraft and equipment to Afghanistan but take over a pool or set of ten helicopters, ground support equipment, vehicles and spares based at Camp Bastion and a series of Forward Arming and Refuelling Points (FARPs). Helicopters and other items are rotated home according to a maintenance and repair schedule that is not synchronized with unit handovers.

The consumption of ammunition is the biggest difference between operations in Afghanistan and routine training in the UK. While in theatre there is considerable difference between consumption of ammunition during routine operations and deliberate operations. The former, consists mainly of small top-ups of weapons but during major operations consumption shoots up. A system of hot refuelling and re-arms is what one AAC officer described as being 'like a Formula 1 pit stop'.

An Afghan veteran recalled:

> On deliberate operations the aircraft come in and out of [landing spots to re-arm] You get used to deliberate ops. We build lanes of ammo next to the spots ready to load on the helicopters when they come back. In the command post we would listen to the battle on the radio and so we can predict when we need to pre-position ammo to re-arm the helicopters.

Weapons statistics for the AH Force released by the Ministry of Defence show the intensity of fighting in Afghanistan. They show that Apache AH.1s fired 183 AGM-114 Hellfire missiles in 2007, compared with 97 in 2008 and 50 up to 24 March in 2009. Consumption of 30mm cannon ammunition

Every Apache pilot has his own helmet valued at $50,000, which can control the helicopter's night vision sensors and 30mm cannon. (Tim Ripley)

is equally heavy with some 29,800 rounds being fired between August and October 2006. In the next six months, the AH Force fired 21,000 rounds of 30mm ammunition. This rose to 27,800 over the next six months, 15,700 in the following six months, 34,400 between April and October 2008 and 43,200 in the six months up to April 2009.

Up to the end of 2009, several UK Apache had been hit by Taliban fire but only one of the helicopters was put out of action. The only major loss was of helicopter ZJ177 in an accident at FOB Edinburgh outside Musa Qalah on 4 September 2009. The aircrew survived and the airframe was air freighted to the UK for repair.

During the summer of 2006, the senior management of the Ministry of Defence's Attack Helicopter Integrated Project Team (AH IPT) at Yeovil were getting increasingly worried by the surge in flying by the eight Apache in Afghanistan. According to the AH IPT leader at the time, Brigadier Nick Knudsen, this level of activity was way above what had been planned and budgeted for. 'When I took over the IPT in 2004 I was told there would be no enduring operations until mid 2009, so we bought spares accordingly,' he said.

On top of this, the maintenance regime for the Apache AH.1 called for each helicopter to go through 'depth maintenance' after 300 hours' flying, involving complete disassembly of the rotor hubs and inspection of all major

Colonel David Turner was the first commander of the AAC's Attack Helicopter Force and had the job of co-ordinating all aspects of Apache AH.1 operations.
(Tim Ripley)

Several Apache AH.1s are held in long-term storage at Wattisham to help sustain the Attack Helicopter Force in business for another two decades. (Tim Ripley)

components. The potential looked high for a 'maintenance train wreck' as Apache returning from Afghanistan stacked up outside maintenance hangars in the UK waiting for their 300 hours' servicing. This would then ripple through the training of other Apache units in UK who were in the process of preparing to deploy to theatre but would have no helicopters to fly.

'Extreme measures' were called for, say AH IPT managers who launched a root and branch review of how UK Apache support was organized and executed. In consultation with the design authority Boeing and its UK prime contractor and co-ordinating design authority AgustaWestland, the servicing regime was changed to extend the time between depth maintenance from 300 to 600 flying hours. Extra spares were purchased to allow the flow rate of airframes through maintenance to be increased.

At the same time the AH DSU at Wattisham was created and lean processes introduced, including the opening of a pulse line. Some 200 civil contractors were hired to augment the military personnel of 7 Air Assault Battalion of the Royal Electrical and Mechanical Engineers (REME) to allow the flow of helicopters through depth maintenance to be increased from twenty to thirty-five per year in 2010. Although it was originally intended to move to this style of support organization for the UK AH Force, the Afghan operation forced the pace of change three years' earlier than expected. The results of these actions meant the AH Force averaged between 800 and 1,100 flying hours a month during 2007.

Defence Logistic Transformation Programme (DLTP) economy measures were also in full swing in 2006 at the time so no major new investment was available to fund modifying the hangar that houses the AH DSU. 'There was no existing organization for dedicated AH support,' Lieutenant Colonel Phil Davies, the Depth Support Manager at the time, recalled. 'It was not a simple exercise – no depth existed as the fleet was not fully fielded. There was no funding line until April 2007. We are constantly running ahead of plans.'

Under the old support set-up groups of REME personnel, supported by Serco technicians, were assigned to a single aircraft and did all the work required on it. This has since been replaced by a classic pulse line where helicopters flow along a line through work stations. 'We have eight pulse stations,' said Davies. 'There is a fifty-two day turn around and we can put thirty-five airframes through per year.'

The Depth Support Unit at Wattisham is the hub of all maintenance of Apache AH.1 helicopters. (Tim Ripley)

Supporting the Apache squadron deployed on operations in Afghanistan is the top priority for Ministry of Defence logistic planners. (Tim Ripley)

Davies continues:

> We have to be clever about whole fleet management. We have to try to take a longer view of the 9,000-hour life of the helicopters. We can't take our eye off the ball and keep our through life head on so we do not fly our helicopters to destruction.

The Apache Integrated Operational Support (AIOS) contract, valued at £439 million for the initial period to March 2014, was announced on 6 October 2009 by the UK Minister of State for Defence Equipment and Support, Quentin Davies MP, during a visit to Wattisham.

The AIOS contract is intended to deliver greater aircraft availability while reducing through life costs by more than £50 million in the initial five-year

205

period and follows from the similar IOS availability-based contracts for the UK's AW101 Merlin and Sea King helicopter fleets. The contract is output-based, whereby AgustaWestland is incentivized to improve the levels of operational output while seeking continuous improvement to reduce through life costs.

Combat operations in Afghanistan have resulted in UK Apache under-going several modifications with urgent operational requirement (UOR) funding. These include long-range communication upgrades and the fitting of armoured CRV-7 rocket pods. This later modification followed several Apache being damaged by Taliban machine gun fire. The most high profile addition was the adoption of the AGM-114N1 Metal Augmented Charge (MAC) variant of the Hellfire, which were fired in anger for the first time in May 2008. Some twenty were fired that year and twenty-three during 2009.

The missiles were purchased with UOR funding after AAC Apache crews in Afghanistan reported in late 2006 that the existing UK inventory of Hellfire high-explosive/fragmentation (HE/frag) and High Explosive Anti-Tank (HEAT) warheads had limited effectiveness against fortified Taliban insurgent positions and walled compounds.

The only major, non-UOR, upgrade of the UK Apache force since it entered service in 2001, has been the incorporation of the Lockheed Martin M-TADS/PNVS (Modernized Target Acquisition Designation Sight/Pilot Night Vision Sensor) along with TEDAC (TADS Electronic Display and Control) systems. Just over forty UK Apache had received the upgrade by late 2009 and in October of that year the last of the modified helicopters required in Afghanistan would be air freighted to theatre.

Britain's Army aviators are now combat hardened by years of operations in Afghanistan. Almost a decade ago, the Apache was at the heart of negative media coverage, with the National Audit Office issuing a highly critical report of its delayed procurement. This is now well and truly a thing of the past and the British Army is clearly getting its money's worth from its Apache helicopters and their crews. 'Sweating the metal' is the buzzword the AAC uses to described its intense utilization of its sixty-seven Apache.

Chapter 14

Lynx Force

O ver the summer of 2010, 9 Regiment Army Air Corps (AAC) began deploying to Afghanistan with the newly upgraded AgustaWestland Lynx AH.9A. The feedback from the pilots and aircraft commanders for the first combat deployment of the upgraded helicopters was universally positive thanks to extra 37 per cent power the AH.9As new LHTEC CTS800-4N engines provided in the hot and high conditions in Afghanistan.

The arrival of the Lynx AH.9A in Afghanistan in May 2010 transformed the capabilities of the AAC light utility helicopter detachment in Afghanistan. (AgustaWestland)

The view of one veteran AAC Lynx pilot after flying the AH.9A for a few months was:

> The engines look after themselves. We have a lot more power so the performance of the helicopter is no longer limited by engine power, we are now only limited by the airframe. With the older Lynx AH.7 that we have used up to now in Afghanistan on dusty landings when you were committed to going in, you are going to land no matter what happens in the dust cloud. You just had no power to overshoot. Now, with the new CTS800-4N engines you always have options.
>
> If you lose one engine, the other one still has enough power to allow you to continue flight to put down safely out of a danger area. If you lost a Gem engine on the older aircraft during your descent, you just had to keep going in. Now you have options, before it was all down to technique and anticipation.
>
> In terms of speed, we are now limited by what you bolt on the outside of the aircraft. Now we have got the same lift capability in the Afghan summer as we have on helicopters in the UK. This is now limited by airframe lift capability, rather than power available. The AH.9A is a significant change up in capability for us.

Lynx AH.7s were the first AAC light utility helicopters in Helmand province in Afghanistan in May 2006. (Tim Ripley)

9 Regiment received the first Lynx AH.9As in late 2009 and then was the first unit to take them to Afghanistan. (Tim Ripley)

The arrival of the Lynx AH.9A has transformed the capabilities of the AAC's light utility helicopter and meant its role in Afghanistan has increased dramatically.

In 2009 the AAC had completed its conversion of all its attack helicopter squadrons to the AgustaWestland Apache AH.1 and its Lynx had been concentrated in two regiments, 1 Regiment AAC at Gütersloh in Germany and 9 Regiment at Dishforth in North Yorkshire. The five light utility helicopter (LUH) squadrons of these two regiments are closely affiliated with the Fleet Air Arm's 847 Naval Air Squadron (NAS), which also operates half a dozen Lynx AH.7s. The AAC LUH regiments operated a mix of around fifteen Lynx AH.7s and twelve AH.9As in late 2010.

Although the British Army deployed its first AgustaWestland Lynx AH.7 to Afghanistan's Helmand province in the summer of 2006, the Central Asian country's high altitude and hot climate meant its performance was severely limited. The AAC was subsequently forced to limit Lynx deployments to Afghanistan's winter months when temperatures had dropped low enough to allow the helicopters to operate effectively during daylight hours.

The Lynx AH.9A is easily recognized by its distinctive engine exhausts. (Tim Ripley)

AAC Lynx crews prepare for a mission over southern Afghanistan in September 2006. (Tim Ripley)

With front-line UK commanders calling for more helicopter support, it was not surprising that the UK Joint Helicopter Command (JHC) and the Defence Equipment & Support Organization, in co-operation with Agusta-Westland, began to look at ways to provide the AAC's Lynx AH.9 with more power.

An urgent operational requirement (UOR) process was set in train to provide the AAC's Lynx AH.9 with new LHTEC CTS800-4N engines and associated FADEC engine control system. This culminated in December 2008 with an announcement by the then Defence Secretary, John Hutton, that the UK Ministry of Defence intended to sign a contract within a few weeks with AgustaWestland to rapidly upgrade twelve British Army Lynx AH.9 aircraft with CTS800-4N engines.

The Lynx AH.9s were selected for the upgrade programme because they were the youngest aircraft in the AAC Lynx fleet, having only been delivered in the early 1990s. These twenty-two aircraft were purchased for utility tasks in support of British Army airmobile brigades and featured a distinctive tricycle undercarriage. They also lacked the TOW missile system fitted to Lynx AH.1s and AH.7s, which made up the bulk of the AAC fleet.

211

The announcement coincided with a renewed commitment by Hutton to the Future Lynx or Lynx Wildcat programme to provide the Army Air Corps and Fleet Air Army with enhanced Lynx helicopters towards the middle of the coming decade. The upgraded AH.9As would pull through the engines and other technology that is intended to be installed on the Wildcat.

Hutton said that the first four of the twelve aircraft, dubbed AH.9As, would be delivered in late 2009 and the remaining eight would be delivered by October 2010. The CTS800-4N engines and associated equipment produce 37 per cent more power than the old Rolls-Royce Gem engines that are fitted to the helicopter giving the new aircraft a significant increase in power.

The first Lynx AH Mk.9A successful maiden flight, which lasted some sixty minutes, took place on 12 November 2009 at AgustaWestland's Yeovil facility. The company commenced work even before the Lynx AH.9A UOR contract award to ensure the programme could be completed as rapidly as possible. A written-off airframe supplied by the Ministry of Defence was used to trial the installation and changes required to the 'top deck' structure of the aircraft, as a risk reduction exercise. Similarly AgustaWestland's

The small fleet of Lynx AH.9As are shared by AAC squadrons preparing to deploy to Afghanistan. (Tim Ripley)

The first Lynx AH.9As were returned to the AAC in late 2009 to allow training to begin for deployments to Afghanistan. (AgustaWestland)

Super Lynx 300 demonstrator aircraft was used to perform a range of trials in support of the programme to speed up the qualification process prior to entry into service. The Lynx AH Mk.9A upgrade comprises the installation of CTS800-4N engines, which require modifications to be carried out to the main gear box, top deck structure and rear fuselage. Additionally changes are carried out in the cockpit where the new FADEC engine controls and digital displays are installed. AgustaWestland is also providing a comprehensive support for the Lynx AH Mk.9A aircraft, including an initial spares package, integrated electronic technical publications and training. The initial training package included training for aircraft and avionic technicians, as well as aircrew and was to be completed by the end of November 2009.

In March 2010 the UK Ministry of Defence announce that it had awarded a £42 million contract extension to the Lynx AH.9A programme for the upgrade of ten more British Army Lynx Mk.9 helicopters with CTS800-4N engines. The contract was announced by the then Minister for Defence Equipment and Support, Quentin Davies MP, during a visit to Agusta-

213

Westland's Yeovil facility. The Minister also accepted delivery of the seventh upgraded Lynx Mk.9A during his visit before handing it over to Lieutenant Colonel Mike McGinty, Commanding Officer of 9 Regiment, the first unit that was scheduled to deploy to Afghanistan with the aircraft. Deliveries of the additional ten Lynx Mk.9A aircraft back to the British Army started during early 2011 and are to be completed in early 2012.

The first Lynx AH.9As were airlifted to Afghanistan in May 2010 on an RAF C-17 Globemaster II strategic transport aircraft and began operations soon afterwards. This represented an eighteen-month timeline from the signing of the Lynx AH.9A contract to the delivery of the first helicopters to the front line in Afghanistan.

In addition to the enhanced engines, the Lynx AH.9A features many improvements to its systems to significantly improve its attack and intelligence, surveillance, target acquisition and reconnaissance (ISTAR) capabilities. This includes twin Rockwell Collins TALON secure radios, Wescam MX-15 electro-optical sensor turret and mountings for M3M 0.50-calibre machine guns capable of firing over 850 rounds per minute. The size of the MX-15 monitor panel and the M3M mounting means that the two systems cannot be used together at the same time.

Images from the MX-15 camera systems used by Lynx AH.9/9As can be displayed on a rugged portable tablet in the helicopter's cockpit. (Tim Ripley)

The Lynx AH.9A's distinctive engine exhausts, tail strakes and MX-15 camera are clearly shown here. (Tim Ripley)

This enhanced performance of the Lynx AH.9A has already significantly improved the operational effectiveness of the AAC detachment in Afghanistan. 'Before we had the AH.9A we only deployed AH.7 to Afghanistan in the winter period from September to March' said Major Al Stocker, officer commanding 659 Squadron AAC. 'Now we have a true 365-day, all year round capability.'

The first AH.9A helicopters, of 672 Squadron, arrived at the main UK helicopter base in Afghanistan, Camp Bastion, in May 2010 and the new helicopters were quickly performing a wide range of front-line tasks, including convoy overwatch, support helicopter escort, reconnaissance and surveillance, and the movement of forces.

Major Stocker, whose squadron replaced 672 Squadron in late July 2010, said the main roles of the Lynx in Afghanistan include moving people and cargo to remote patrol bases that are urgently needed. An important role of MX-15-equipped Lynx is convoy overwatch, which involves flying

215

All AAC Lynx helicopters undergo deep maintenance at Vector Aerospace's facility at Fleetlands in Hampshire. (Tim Ripley)

ahead or on the flanks of road convoys looking for improvised explosive devices, groups of insurgents or other threats. The camera is also used for reconnaissance tasks.

Deputy Commander of 672 Squadron, Captain Pete Marfleet, recalled in July 2010 that his Lynx crews could track insurgent movements and overwatch vulnerable areas with its sophisticated surveillance camera.

This overwatch capability helps with the protection of the massive convoys used to resupply front-line troops in the forward operating bases.

The convoys can be vulnerable to attack as they track across vast swathes of desert from base to base but with the Lynx circling above, the insurgents usually stay away.

Captain Marfleet commented:

> I'd be concerned if we had lots of contacts every time we flew a mission. Success for us means we've got a convoy or a support helicopter in and out of a patrol base without any trouble. Just our presence in the overhead and the threat from our weapons systems means that the enemy wisely keep their heads down.

In combat operations the Lynx provides both an offensive and a 'Command and Control' capability, said Captain Marfleet, by operating overhead and directing the battle or providing the force commander with a bird's-eye view of what's happening on the ground.

Since it was first used on Lynx AH.7s and AH.9s in Iraq, the AAC has built up considerable expertise using the MX-15 camera system to monitor complex ground combat situations. AAC aircrewmen say the system requires considerable expertise to get the best from it. 'The aircraft commander has a remote tablet that he can use to look at the camera images' said a AAC aircrewman.

> The commander talks the MX-15 operator on to target. It is not easy to do. It is good if operator and commander work regularly together as a formed crew and they know the area they are operating in. It is very disorientating when you are the helicopter back cabin because you have no way to orientate yourself to the outside world. On one exercise the operator even thought he was looking at a target 180 degrees off beam, he though the target was in front of the aircraft when it was actually right behind it.

M3M-equipped Lynx are now used to escort troop-carrying Agusta-Westland Merlin and Boeing Chinook HC.2 helicopters. 'Now we have an offensive capability we can effectively fire back and take over some escort work' said Stocker. 'We can also do close combat attack.'

Stocker said the AAC got good feedback from 672 Squadron who had taken the Lynx AH.9A to Afghanistan for the first time. 'We have the most powerful power-to-weight ratio in theatre,' he said. 'It is a quantum leap forward for Lynx aircrew.'

Major Max Lytle, Officer Commanding of 672 Squadron, the first Lynx AH.9 unit to deploy, commented, 'We are playing an important role in protecting our ground forces and carrying out surveillance, boosting performance in Afghanistan's challenging conditions.'

9 Regiment aircrews undertook extensive pre-deployment flight training on the new aircraft in Kenya to gain flying experience in similar 'hot and high' conditions before the start of their first operational tours in the Lynx Mk.9A. Earlier in 2010, 672 Squadron joined 4th Mechanized Brigade for its mission rehearsal exercise on Salisbury Plain before it deployed to Afghanistan in April and May.

As the next AH.9A unit to go out to theatre, 659 Squadron went through a Mission Specific Training (MST) package, dubbed Exercise Demon's Quest, in May and June organized by 9 Regiment. This put the crews through Afghan-specific standard operating procedures, tactics and drills.

The AAC Lynx fleet is to be augmented by the Lynx Wildcat in 2014. (AgustaWestland)

Stocker recalled:

> The idea of this is that the culmination exercise, which pulls together all the individual training packages together – calls for fire, tactical pairs flying, etc. This exercise is the opportunity to pull everything in together in one sortie, adding complexity or 'treacle'. We have added the airspace management procedures that aircrew get in theatre, as well as the special instructions and the call signs used in theatre. We replicate the Joint HF(A) command set up, so crews are given the tasking sheets, infra-structure and engineering support they will find in theatre. The guys all plan and fly a mission as they would in Afghanistan.

AAC commanders have established a force rotation cycle of their Lynx squadrons to sustain a detachment of around five of the newly upgraded AgustaWestland Lynx AH.9As in Afghanistan for when new Lynx Wildcat helicopters are set to replace them from 2014.

218

A pool of twelve of the Lynx AH.9As is shared around the AAC's two LUH regiments and 847 Naval Air Squadron on a rolling basis. At any one time around four or five of the helicopters with LHTEC CTS800-4N engines are at Camp Bastion supporting the UK's JHF(A), four are in the UK for use in pre-deployment training and the remaining three are expected to be undergoing depth maintenance at Vector Aerospace's Fleetlands site in Hampshire at any one time. The UK ordered ten additional Lynx AH.9As, which will be operated outside this cycle by another unit.

In 2010, the three Lynx squadrons of 9 Regiment AAC based at Dishforth in North Yorkshire had the Afghan commitment and deployed their first Lynx AH.9A equipped sub-unit, 672 Squadron, to Afghanistan in April 2010 and their replacement, 659 Squadron, then completed its pre-deployment training ahead for moving to Afghanistan towards the end of July 2010.

According to Major Stocker, 'there will be a rolling hand over process for the Lynx AH.9A'. He said the regiment operated a mix of older legacy four AH.7s and five AH.9 Lynx and three of the new Lynx AH.9As. Once 659 Squadron had completed its training, personnel from the regiment's remaining sub-unit, 669 Squadron, took over the Lynx AH.9As for training ahead of their deployment in October/November 2010.

Stocker said:

> We will then hand over the AH.9A to 847 Naval Air Squadron [at Yeovilton Naval Air Station in Somerset] in November for their Afghanistan training. They will pass them onto 1 Regiment AAC [in Germany], which has 661 and 652 Squadron, in 2011 to begin their Afghanistan pre-deployment training. Then we will go back to being a legacy AH.7 only regiment. In October 2011 we will get the AH.9A back and start deploying again. We will just have AH.7s when we are outside our operational commitment period.

By early 2011, the AAC's Lynx Force was fully committed to the campaign in Afghanistan for the foreseeable future. Its new Lynx AH.9As have given the venerable Lynx a new lease of life and chart a path for the LUH capability until the Lynx Wildcat arrives.

Chapter 15

Keeping the AAC Flying

To sustain its AH forces in the field the AAC has had to build up a deployable logistic support capability that meets the demanding technical requirements of modern helicopters and this has drawn on its tried and tested logistic principles.

In August 2009 664 Squadron AAC deployed to the North of England to support Exercise Lightning Force and this showed off how the AAC supports its helicopters in the field. The squadron was tasked with providing the 'framework' support for a conversion-to-role (CTR) course being run by the Air Manoeuvre Training and Advisory Team (AMTAT) using the Spadeadam Electronic Warfare Training Ranges. As a secondary task it had to provide aircraft to participate in a combined arms live fire exercise (CALFEX) on Otterburn Training Area.

The hub of this activity was a disused former World War Two airfield within the Albermarle Barracks complex, a few miles to the north of Newcastle-upon-Tyne. The squadron had set up a deployed operating base alongside the old concrete taxi ways to support eight Apache and a single Eurocopter Squirrel HT1s from the Defence Helicopter Flying School, which was used as an exercise control aircraft. Some 150 personnel, including some fifty Royal Electrical Mechanical Engineers (REME) technicians and fifty AAC flight line operations personnel, deployed to Albermarle Barracks from 4 Regiment AAC's main operating base at Wattisham in Suffolk.

This type of deployment had become routine for the AAC's six AH squadrons when they were not on operations in Afghanistan. Almost every major UK exercise run by the British Army, as well as many Royal Marines and Royal Air Force exercises, involves some sort of AH participation and that entails a logistic support package being deployed. The majority of these are pre-deployment or mission rehearsal exercises (MRE) for units heading to Afghanistan. A typical UK brigade pre-deployment work-up for Afghanistan – of which there are two cycles a year – can involve a two-week long full brigade MRE, up to half a dozen smaller battlegroup MREs and a number of CALFEXs, all requiring AH support.

At the end of the flight line, 664 Squadron's Close Support Section had set up shop to keep the aircraft deployed on the exercise flying. It deployed on the exercise with fifty-one personnel from the Royal Electrical and Mechanical Engineers (REME), Royal Logistics Corps (RLC) and Royal Air Force (RAF), which its officer commanding, Warrant Officer Class 2 (Artificer Quarter-master Sergeant) Craig People, said was typical for this type of training event. The section is one of three from 4 Regiment's REME workshop and each of its three flying squadrons has a section permanently attached.

He said thirty-two personnel were his own technicians and ten were temporarily assigned from 7 Battalion, REME, at Wattisham, which normally provides 2nd Line Support to the AH Force, 'Out of the 51, two are RAF,

Forward Arming and Refuelling Points (FARPs) manned by the AAC's ground personnel keep its helicopter flying and fighting. (Tim Ripley)

The AAC regularly operates it helicopters close to the front lines so it is not dependent on fixed airbases. (Tim Ripley)

three RLC. The rest are REME avionics and aircraft technicians' said People. 'They also include one armourer and two vehicle mechanics.'

At the heart of the REME Section's operation is a deployable spares pack loaded onto four large trucks.

> The packs contents are pre-programmed and we look at usage over time to decide what goes in it. Three RLC suppliers run it on a twenty-four-hour basis. To get additional spares they are hooked up on a secure internet server in the Ministry of Defence and they can look in the main stores inventory. If we have an aircraft that goes 'AOG' or 'aircraft on ground' then a civilian courier service will get us spares here within 24 hours. We have had couriers arriving at main gate here at 2 a.m. in the morning.

The rest of the REME operation took places in a series of large tents, as well as a tooling truck and an office truck with all the section's aircraft publications installed on a number of ruggedised secure laptop computers.

People said:

> Apache likes the heat. When we bring it up here in January and February for exercises the helicopter does not like the wet. It likes deserts and works well in them. Today, for example, because it is misty and damp I have my guys out working on the flight line because we known there will be things for them to do. Serviceability has been good here. Out of eight Apache, every day we have six working and on some days had eight.
>
> We do repairs to the aircraft in theatre. The Royal Navy Mobile Aircraft Support Unit (MASU) is in Afghanistan to do battle damage repair and they do all the metal and composite repairs.

Battle damage is quite common in Afghanistan, including a rocket launcher that was shot up in 2007 and had to be jettison. A main rotor blade has been shot through and pilots did not even notice until they go back to base. The

The pre-positioning of ammunition and other weapons at FARPs ensures that AAC Apache AH.1s are always ready whenever they are called into action. (Tim Ripley)

Repairing AAC helicopters at forward operating bases is the job of the Royal Electrical and Mechanical Engineers (REME). (Tim Ripley)

Depth Support Unit at Wattisham always has one or two helicopters that have been shot up, he said.

People said:

> I have been working on aircraft for eighteen years – Lynx, Gazelle, Islanders and Defenders. We have a good spread of experience on the Apache. You quickly forget things on AH. We have just finished working on the flight line at Wattisham so we got up to speed on running faults. Up here on exercise we have had got to get back quickly up to speed on the weapons side.
>
> It is good running a section. I look forward to going on operations. Since being on AH I like to go to work. It is always a busy day at work. There is no slacking in the AH Force. To keep on top of your game you have got to work hard. You have got to push the guys hard at times.

The day-to-day operations on 664 Squadron's flight line were the responsibility of its Ground Support Flight. This was manned by senior non-commissioned officers and soldiers or air troopers of the AAC.

224

The flight line operation was very basic, with the aircraft arming teams working from a 9×9 tent on the edge of the hard standing. In between launching and recovering aircraft they had to refuel and re-arm the helicopters.

The flight's second-in-command, Staff Sergeant Ronnie Barker, said that there were six arming teams in each squadron, each is seven strong and run by a corporal or experienced lance corporal, as section commander known as Arming and Loading Point Controllers. Within a section, two pairs of soldiers control two landing spots on a forward arming and refuelling (FARP), while the remaining three soldiers run a base location, monitoring radios and aircraft paperwork. On Exercise Lightning Force, the flight split itself into two shifts due to the requirement to run night flight operations.

AAC flight personnel are multi-skilled and they are trained to carry out arming, refuelling, as well as launching and recovering helicopters. In addition, more than a dozen AAC personnel provide signallers and drivers for the squadron command post.

Since May 2006, the main operational commitment of the AAC has been sustaining a squadron-sized detachment of ten Apache AH.1s in Afghanistan.

'We work with a squadron all next year and then go on operations' said People. 'We deploy in May 2010 and are back in UK by September. When we finish in Afghanistan, we come home and start training again' commented one air trooper.'

Faults on the Apache AH.1 are diagnosed by computers. (Tim Ripley)

WOII Craig People ran the 664 Squadron's Close Support Section in 2009 and was responsible for ensuring its helicopters were ready for action in Afghanistan. (Tim Ripley)

People said:

> Afghanistan will be the culmination of our training. It is part of the eighteen-month 'form cycle'. The 'form cycle' means there is new blood in the section. It would be hard work if no one moved. You need to change the dynamics of the group. After operations we end our tour cycle. The aircraft is ideal for Afghanistan and it is good to see it being used. It is an invaluable bit of kit out there and it is good to see it doing the business.

UK AH squadrons do not deploy with their own aircraft and equipment to Afghanistan but take over a pool or set of ten helicopters, ground support equipment, vehicles and spares based at Camp Bastion. These items are rotated home according to a maintenance and repair schedule that is not synchronized with unit handovers. People said:

> When we go to Afghan we take over kit already there, things stay in place. On Operation Herrick, the survival equipment guys from the RAF and RLC suppliers are rotated on a separate basis. All my technicians, vehicle mechanics and armourers are part of the equipment support package. We take over kit and vehicles out there in Afghanistan. This includes a 'white fleet' for use in camp (4 × 4s and vans) and green fleet for going out on the ground. All UK AH are based at Bastion but we do have the capacity to work at FARPs

All spares and tools to keep an AAC Attack Helicopter squadron flying and fighting are carried in several four tons trucks. (Tim Ripley)

and forward operating bases if operations require it. In Afghanistan in 2007, I was forward based for three weeks. That was the only time in the four months I was there. There is no change to aircraft servicing policies out there, except for climate related issues. The only difference is the climate and our living accommodation.

To prepare AAC squadrons for Afghan tours a period of pre-deployment training (PDT) is undertaken for six weeks in the US, under the banner of Exercise Crimson Eagle. 664 Squadron's PDT took place from October to December 2009 ahead of its Afghan tour in May 2010. People recalled:

We did weapons and live firing in the heat and dust to get up to speed for Afghanistan. Then we did exercises in the UK in January and February 2010 with other deploying units. Then we went to Afghanistan after we had done everything 100%.

Barker said:

The way we train on all our exercises is aimed at war. We play as we go out there. We work the same way every day. The strongest thing out there in Afghanistan is the time life of ammunition. All the paperwork is done by the ammunition SNCO. We try to rotate ammunition through Afghanistan, so it is reconditioned and has a lifespan. Ammunition always has to be top notch. We would not put old rockets on an aircraft in case they do not fire. Annual servicing keeps kit at top notch.

The consumption of ammunition is the biggest difference between operations in Afghanistan and routine training in the UK, according to AAC air troopers. While in theatre there is considerable difference between consumption of ammunition during routine operations and deliberate operations. The former consists mainly of small top-ups of weapons but during major operations consumption shoots up. A system of hot refuelling and re-arming was once described by an AAC officer as being 'like a Formula 1 pit stop'.
 An Afghan veteran said:

On deliberate operations the aircraft come in and out of [landing spots to re-arm]. You get used to deliberate ops. We build lanes of ammo next to the spots ready to load on the helicopters when they come back. In the command post we listen to the battle on the radio and so we can predict when we need to pre-position ammo to re-arm the helicopters.

During deliberate operations it is also increasingly common for FARPs to be set up in UK FOBs, such as FOB Robinson, Dwyer and Edinburgh, on the outer fringes of Helmand provinces. 'More and more we are going to out stations,' said one AAC Afghan veteran. These deployments are often conducted by helicopter with ground crews, fuel and weapons moved by RAF Chinook to FOBs.

There are many veterans in 664 Squadron of the early AH deployments to Afghanistan in 2006 and they report considerable differences to that period. Barker said:

> Between May and September 2006 Bastion has evolved and welfare has evolved. They have started to make the place better. You also see a difference in what senior commanders are trying to achieve. You never know what the aircraft are going to do.

A female AAC Lance Corporal described the situation in Afghanistan in 2006 'as more up in the air'. 'We did not have a lot of kit in Bastion,' she said. 'It was sparse. This time there are a lot more amenities.'

One of her male colleagues complained that too much emphasis on welfare amenities can have a detrimental effect on the fighting edge of British troops, describing the former AH main operating base at Kandahar Airfield as 'a

Giant Oshkosh tankers now provide fuel for AAC helicopters in the UK and on operations overseas. (Tim Ripley)

holiday camp'. He made the telling point that while overall welfare facilities had increased by 20 per cent since 2006 there was still 'not enough ping pong balls at Camp Bastion'.

Logistic support in the AAC's Lynx regiments and squadrons is carried out very differently from the methods used in the AH Force. Major changes began during 2009 saw moves away from holding engineering, motor transport and other support capabilities at squadron level to centralizing them at regimental level.

The AAC's 9 Regiment, based at Dishforth in North Yorkshire, has been at the forefront of these developments, which are expected to lay the foundations for the support concept for the new AgustaWestland Lynx Wildcat light utility helicopter (LUH) when it enters service in 2014.

Previously, AAC Lynx squadrons had their own integral Royal Electrical and Mechanical Engineer (REME) close support section permanently attached, along with motor transport, radio communicators and administrative staff. Now these personnel and their associated equipment are held by at regiment level and are distributed to squadrons for specific training exercises or operational deployments.

Apache AH.1 helicopters are returned to the Depth Support Unit at Wattisham after several months on duty in Afghanistan to be dismantled, cleaned, overhauled and re-assembled. (Tim Ripley)

Major Al Stocker said:

> When I took command of 659 Squadron in 2007 I had seventy-four
> people. Now I have twenty-four people – twenty-one aircrew, a
> squadron sergeant major, a squadron quarter master sergeant and
> one administrator. We used to have signals, motor transport and
> engineers within the squadron, now they are centralized in the
> Regiment's Manoeuvre Support Squadron and the command and
> signals group. The REME Workshop controls all the engineers.

Stocker's squadron put the new support concept to the test during a
deployment from Dishforth to a training area within Marne Barrack in
Catterick in June 2010 to establish a forward operating location to conduct
pre-deployment training ahead of a tour in Afghanistan later in the year. Co-
ordinating the engineering support for the exercise, Artificer Quartermaster
Sergeant (AQMS) Will Watchorn, of 9 Regimental Workshop, described the
new way of working.

> Each squadron of the regiment's three squadrons used to have close
> support section, with its own hangar, engineer officer who worked
> for the squadron officer commanding. We could deploy complete
> on exercises and operations. We were embedded in squadron with
> our own aircraft and tools.

A mix of civilian contractors and military personnel work at Wattisham's Depth
Support Unit to keep the Attack Helicopter Force flying. (Tim Ripley)

There are not enough aircraft, tools and technicians to go around to man three squadrons to the old way. Aircraft, people and tools are pooled and resource-based. Now we have gone to the forward and echelon concept. The forward organization does the flying side with squadrons. Echelon does big things – major servicings such as changing engines and gear boxes.

The Artificer Sergeant Major in the workshop decides who mans exercise and operational detachments. He is a sort of fleet manager, who calls the shots on who goes where. He picks people who deploy with the squadrons. When we designate people to go on Operation Herrick [in Afghanistan], we align them with that squadron some time ahead so they go with the same squadron on exercises beforehand. That way they can get to know the aircraft and detachment commanders. From the management point of view you have to adapt, improvise, overcome. That is what we are paid for – we make it work.

659 Squadron was preparing to deploy to Afghanistan in July 2010 and was the second AAC sub-unit to take the new Lynx AH.9A, with upgraded LHTEC CTS800-4N engines and FADEC engine control system, on operations. Watchorn said the engineer support requirements for the upgraded helicopter are greater than the older model of Lynx. In 2010, the 9 Regiment's REME Workshop had some twenty-six people deployed to Camp Bastion to support the four aircraft strong Lynx AH.9A detachment.

'The engineering requirement is big' Watchorn said. 'The AH.9A requires fifteen maintenance hours for each flying hour. This should come down as we become more familiar with the aircraft and get more spares.'

The rapid introduction of the Lynx AH.9A under the urgent operational requirement process had led to an increased training requirement, he said.

Although the Lynx AH.9A upgrade is not a complete re-build, it has not gone through a three to four year in-service process to iron out many minor technical issues and get the supply chain fully up and running, claim AAC and REME personnel. '9 Regiment is the first unit to use the helicopter and hopefully we will sort out the issues,' said a senior REME technician.

Watchorn said:

We are the second REME section to get aircraft. We did an equipment course at [AgustaWestland at] Yeovil for five to seven days on avionics and aircraft air frames. Then we did augmented training within our unit to certify people, so they are cleared to sign off the aircraft. This is a big training burden for us.

Field servicing on a Lynx AH.9 by a REME technician. (Tim Ripley)

AAC ground crew are multi-skilled at arming, refuelling and repairing helicopters in field conditions. (Tim Ripley)

Stocker said that the experience operating and supporting the Lynx AH.9A would provide the basis for the introduction of the Lynx Wildcat. He said of the AAC's other LUH unit, 1 Regiment based in Germany, '1 Regiment is moving to follow us – we are the trial.'

Chapter 16

The Training Pipeline

In a cramped tent on the edge of a Northumbrian pine forest, student air-crew are being briefed on their mission for the day. A few hundred metres away on an old disused World War Two runway within the boundaries of the Royal Artillery's Albermarle Barracks complex, ground crews are making their final checks to eight AgustaWestland Apache AH.1 attack helicopters.

This is Exercise Lightning Force, the culmination of a two-week exercise flying into a hornet's nest of simulated anti-aircraft defence on the UK's Spadeadam Electronic Warfare Training Ranges, astride the Cumbria-Northumberland border. On their missions into the ranges the student Apache aircrew have dodged anti-aircraft guns, manportable surface-to-air missiles or Manpads and bigger radar-guided missiles. 'The Royal Air Force guys who run Spadeadam get very competitive and really make us work hard,' commented student Apache pilot, Captain Rob Gittoes. According to instructors from the Air Manoeuvre Training and Advisory Team (AMTAT), who run the seven and a half month long Conversion-to-Role (CTR) training course, most of the seventeen students on the course will be flying combat missions in the central Asian country a few months after they complete the final phase of their CTR and pre-deployment training (PDT) in United States.

On 1 September 2003, the first front-line British Army pilots began conversion training to fly the AgustaWestland Apache AH.1 at the School of Army Aviation at Middle Wallop. This marked a major milestone in the history of the Army Air Corps (AAC) and was a major achievement in the effort to provide the British Army with an attack helicopter capability.

The war in Afghanistan has pushed the AAC into the public limelight and its helicopter crews are now household names thanks to the dramatic books by retired Apache pilot Ed Macy. When HRH Prince Harry volunteered to begin training as an AAC pilot in 2008, the media profile of the AAC sky rocketed. After the twenty-five-year-old prince successfully gained his pro-visional 'wings' in May 2010 he began conversion training to fly the Apache and if successful in his training he will be ready to deploy to Afghanistan with his squadron in 2012.

The route to becoming a AAC Apache is not easy as Prince Harry found out when he started to learn to fly the attack helicopter in July 2010. Unlike the other two UK armed services, not all AAC pilots are officers and more than half of its pilots are non-commissioned officers (NCOs). The AAC does recruit officers and soldiers, both male and female, direct from civilian life and they undergo initial military training wearing its distinctive light blue beret, before moving onto flying training.

For many years, the AAC has offered officers from other army regiments or corps the chance to serve on attachment after completing flying training. They then have the opportunity to remain in the AAC after completing a two to three-year tour before or to return to their parent unit. NCOs from other regiments, with the minimum rank of lance corporal, can also join the AAC and then re-badge once being awarded their Army Flying Wings.

The initial training for all pilots who are selected for the AAC is the same, irrespective of the helicopter that pilots will ultimately go on to fly and

AAC aircrew have to complete one of the most intensive flight training regimes in the world. (Tim Ripley)

Aspiring AAC pilots start their basic helicopter training flying the Eurocopter Squirrel HT.1 at the Defence Helicopter Flying School at RAF Shawbury. (FBS Heliservices)

command. This phase begins with an initial aptitude test carried out at RAF Cranwell in Lincolnshire. Here the candidates are required to complete a series of computer-based tests to evaluate their suitability and aptitude for flying. At RAF Cranwell the candidates will undergo an initial medical to establish if they are fit to fly helicopters.

On successful completion of both the aptitude test and medical, candidates will arrive at Middle Wallop to carry out what is termed Flying Grading. This is conducted over a period of three to four weeks. If the candidates pass Flying Grading they are then in a position to start the Army Pilots Course (APC).

The Army Pilots Course is approximately eighteen months long and consists of several different phases. The initial phase is conducted in conjunction

237

with both candidates from the Royal Navy and Royal Air Force and includes instruction on elementary flying training on light aircraft. Successful students will then move from RAF Cranwell down to RAF Shawbury to begin rotary aircraft training.

This begins with a period of ground school to bring the students up to speed on the aircraft upon which they will be training. Successful completion of this phase will see the students move through to the School of Army Aviation at Middle Wallop for the final phase that teaches the students how to operate their aircraft in a military environment.

Having completed all the phases the students will be presented with their Army Flying Wings and the pilots are then required to undergo the Conversion to Type (CTT) Courses on the Gazelle, Lynx or Apache AH.1. Candidates for Apache AH.1 training must satisfy additional selection criteria. These criteria consider rank, experience, the arm or service within the armed forces and further medical requirements. The conversion course for the Apache AH.1 consists of two main phases: namely the CTT and the

Conversion to type training on the Apache AH.1 takes place at the Army Aviation Centre at Middle Wallop. (AgustaWestland)

AAC Apache AH.1 pilots must gain an instinctive feel for flying their helicopter.
(Tim Ripley)

Once AAC Apache AH.1 pilots have mastered flying their helicopter they must learn how to fly as a pair with another helicopter. (Tim Ripley)

Conversion To Role (CTR). The CTT focuses on individual training and is six months long.

Aircrew CTT training, as well as ground crew and maintenance personnel training, carried out in co-operation with the Aviation Training International Limited (ATIL) private finance initiative (PFI) company, under a £1.05 billion contract. It has a large presence at the School of Army Aviation at Middle Wallop where the main conversion to type training for aircrew takes place. Many of its 110 personnel have service backgrounds to give the training a 'military feel' and senior AAC staff work side by side with ATIL staff. Twelve Apache are based at Middle Wallop for use by the Army School of Aviation for training and operational evaluation.

ATIL is responsible for providing full mission simulator services at Wattisham in Suffolk for continuation training of squadron air crew. ATIL also provides mobile deployable simulators that can be moved to exercise areas in the UK or on operations overseas for use as mission rehearsal tools. Some 550 AAC personnel pass through ATIL facilities each year.

AAC ground crew begin training at Middle Wallop on how to operate and service Apache in purpose-built class room facilities fitted with advanced inter-active training aids. Royal Electrical Mechanical and Electrical (REME) maintenance personnel are trained on comparable facilities at Arborfield.

AAC ground crew undergo initial military training at the Army Training Regiment at Winchester before moving to Middle Wallop to learn how to re-arm and refuel Army helicopters and also take on other responsibilities. All AAC soldiers are trained to drive and service the Land Rovers and large vehicles used by the AAC, including the 15,000-litre Tactical Air Refueller and the Demountable Rack Offload and Pickup System (DROPS), a 15-tonne flatbed. AAC communication specialists learn how to provide essential communications to both aircraft and other Army ground units. There is also the opportunity to train as an Aviation Support Specialist. This involves preparing loads for air delivery, controlling tactical landing sites and the storage and maintenance of supplies and munitions.

Since the AAC first got its hands on the Apache in 2001, it has worked at a frenetic pace to train air and ground crews to operate the UK version of the Boeing AH-64D Longbow Apache. A training programme or pipeline was set up that involves prospective UK Apache aircrew training and begins at the Army Aviation Centre at Middle Wallop in Hampshire or, as it is known to student pilots, 'The Factory'. This trains aircrew how to actually fly the Apache, use its weapon systems and gain an insight into some basic tactical drills and procedures. According to Gittoes, 'You are trained to be a AH crew member. This is focused on flying as a pair of aircraft.'

This phase is then followed by a seven and a half month long CTR course, which is aimed at bringing crews up to limited combat ready (LCR) status. This is defined as being fit to go war except for brief theatre specific PDT requirements, such as environmental and live fire refresher training. From 2003 to early 2009, CTR courses where focused on converting whole AAC squadrons at a time from the Lynx AH.7 and Westland Gazelle AH.1 to the Apache.

The commitment of the UK Attack Helicopter (AH) Force to combat operations in Afghanistan in 2006 gave added impetuous to the drive to train all its personnel up to a combat ready status. AH crews from 9 Regiment AAC deployed to Helmand Province in southern Afghanistan before the full Force of six AH squadrons were fully converted, further adding to the pressure on the AH training pipeline.

The need now to conduct PDT for every Apache squadron heading to Afghanistan meant that a new series of rolling PDT packages had to be developed. The first squadrons deploying to Afghanistan carried out the main element of their PDT in Oman but this subsequently was switched to the Arizona desert. AMTAT is closely involved in these activities and synchronized them with its own CTR courses to make best use of training time and resources in the US.

241

The last AH unit, 653 Squadron, completed its CTR in April 2009 and since then, AMTAT began running courses with students direct from CTT. This involved making use of 'pool' resources at the AAC main operating base at Wattisham in Suffolk and for Exercise Lightning Force in August 2009 a

Full motion Apache AH.1 simulators are operated by the ATIL consortium on AAC bases at Wattisham and Middle Wallop. (ATIL)

Night flying the Apache AH.1 is a core skill for all AAC Attack Helicopter pilots. (AgustaWestland)

framework unit, 664 Squadron, provided aircraft, vehicles, maintenance, ground support, command and control. At the same time as it was supporting the CTR course, 664 Squadron's own crews were also flying live fire missions from Albermarle to Otterburn Training Area in support of a combined arms live fire exercise for troops of 11 Light Brigade ahead of their own deployment to Afghanistan in September 2009. The squadron also provided the frame work unit for the final phase of the CTR in the United States. As well as providing the physical infrastructure for the exercise, the use of a front-line AH squadron gave students a feel for working from a deployed operating base in a realistic environment.

The CTR is seven and a half months' long and progressively built up the expertise and experience of students. According to Gittoes:

> CTR involves a first phase of conventional patrol drills, then we do simulated Operation Herrick tactics, training and procedures (TTP) as an introduction to Afghanistan operations. The electronic warfare (EW) phase – Lightning Force – is back to conventional operations. Then we do Exercise Crimson Eagle in the States that involves everything we have covered in the course.

243

Major Alex Godfrey, the Senior Flying Instructor at AMTAT, said the EW phase involves students each flying a total of twelve battle and patrol drills or sorties, nine sorties beforehand and the final three on Lightning Force. On these the students fly as crews with instructors.

After completing the sorties at Spadeadam, the students move on to fly twelve more patrol drill sorties; nine of them involve flying against targets on airfields in Suffolk. On these the students fly as formed crews. 'Then we move to the US where they fly three battle and three patrol sorties,' said Godfrey.

Prior to Lightning Force the students flew three simulated sorties in the ATIL simulators at Wattisham. 'This introduces us in slow time to the environment, exposes us to the EW threat and counter-measures,' said Gittoes. 'Once we have passed that we fly real sorties and come on this exercise.'

The three Lightning Force sorties are also progressively more difficult and complex. In the first sortie the students get exposure to simulated weapons used on the Spadeadam ranges, including the so-called 'smokey SAM' rockets, which simulate the exhaust plume of a manpad, the Malina infra-red (IR) simulator that 'excites' the missile warning devices on helicopters to make them think a manpad is heading towards them. The Apache and other exercise players are equipped with laser-based collective training systems so friendly and enemy forces weapon systems engagements can be realistically simulated. 'This phase gives us exposure to seeing the threats being fired,' said Gittoes. 'We react with flares to the IR threats'.

On the second sorties students are exposed to realistic radar threats to activate the helicopter's radar warning devices and Gittoes said they now had to react with chaff and manoeuvre to keep their aircraft safe.

> We learn to react appropriately – it takes a lot of work to achieve this.
>
> On the third sortie we deal with all the threats in a tactical scenario. We fly in a four ship patrol into the area of operations. In planning before the sortie we identify likely enemy locations and establish battle positions to engage enemy threats. The enemy then fight back and the battle develops. We move, utilizing chaff, flares and manoeuvre, staying as low as possible. We keep going until we have defeated the enemy and even refuel at forward arming and refuelling point (FARP) before returning to the engagement.

After the Lightning Force missions, the students and instructors debrief their missions using video recordings from the helicopter's sensors. Gittoes continues:

Extensive use of simulators allows AAC pilots to rehearse missions prior to major exercises or overseas missions. (ATIL)

The co-pilot operates the sensors and in the rear seat the pilot is concentrating on the outside view. During the debrief the crew can interact, swap information about what the other guy saw and was doing during the mission.

These missions are designed to teach students how to cope with reacting to multiple weapons threats and warning alarms when the aircraft is being 'painted' by enemy radar and under attack from manpads. Godfrey said:

Everybody feels they are just keeping their head above water – that is normal. There is a huge amount of information coming into the cockpit – only just a fraction of it important. Only a few people can prioritize that information and still function – continue to manage the situation. The workload is intense.

When they get their first defensive aides system (DAS) warning alarm the reaction is to panic and then pretty soon they have nine alarms going off. We look to see if they process the information, work out what is key and what to put to one side. Also we look at attention to detail, about how they use their systems and sensors.

But Godfrey was also keen to stress that the students still had to press on with the missions aggressively, even when under attack from the enemy.

I want to develop a hunting instinct for targets. So when they pull the trigger they are putting down a precise but sustained weight of fire so they destroy the target completely. In CTR we put a lot of emphasis on building a direct fire plan. When they decide to fire they must completely destroy the target with the weight of fire required. We want a killer instinct but it must be precise, not just point and aim. There are rules of engagement (ROE) and collateral damage limitations to consider. The premium is on controlled aggression. The ROE sometimes do not allow us to prosecute targets. We have to understand what is legally acceptable, it is important to stay legal. We teach a lot about ROE. It is the bread and butter in theatre.

In the wake of Lightning Force in 2009, the seventeen students returned to Wattisham to fly a series of nine more patrol drills or sorties in the East Anglia region, conducting simulates attacks on military sites and airfields in the region. These, however, were then flown by formed crews of students rather than the student/instructor combination used in the early phases of the course.

Only the top student pilots eventually qualify to fly the Apache AH.1. (Tim Ripley)

The finale of CTR was Exercise Crimson Eagle for eight weeks of intense flying on the Barry M Goldwater range complex in the US, under the direction of the AMTAT instructors.

Upon arrival at Crimson Eagle the CTR aircrew undertake four days of environmental qualification (EQ) and hot-and-high instruction. This is followed by four days of day-mountain and night-mountain flying, seven days' range work, five days combined-arms tactical and air-ground fire-support simulator training and 'live' tactics, training and five days' procedural instruction. They then undertake four days of survival and evasion training before embarking on the seven-day long 'Lightning Hurdle' exercise, which embraces all the skills they have learned up to that point and, at the end of which, students are designated as LCR. At the end of the CTR exercise schedule is a proportion of the PDT training events required by aircrew from the operational Apache squadrons preparing to deploy, including extensive live firing.

One of the major elements of Crimson Eagle is joint live fire training with forward air controllers (FACs) or joint terminal attack controllers (JTACs) and members of British Army fire-support teams (FSTs) attached to the ground units from the brigade due to be deployed in Afghanistan at the same time as the Apache crews. United States F-16C/D and A-10C strike jets, UH-60 Blackhawk, UH-1Ys, and AH-1Ws plus AH-64A/D helicopters are also regular participants in Crimson Eagle.

In 2010 the Crimson Eagle exercise series underwent considerable change with a third exercise being added to allow more PDT training to be conducted. The AAC also moved it to the Naval Air Facility El Centro in California, which the RAF is already using to train its AgustaWestland Merlin HC.3 helicopter crews.

Even though the six AH squadrons are now fully converted, the AH Force was still twelve short of its target of 100 fully qualified and current Apache aircrew in March 2010. AMTAT is running 'hot' to get these extra aircrew trained, although the current head of AMTAT, Lieutenant Colonel Yori Griffiths, said that this is very much a 'moving target', as personnel finish tours in AH squadrons, move to different jobs or leave the service. The AH Force is, however, closing on the target with a steady build up of trained personnel. Seventeen aircrew were due to graduate at the end of the 2009 course with a further eighteen students starting CTR training in October and twenty more following in July 2010.

'There will always be a residual requirement for people to come through the [training] system' said Griffiths. 'In 2010 and 2011 we will continue to train at these rates by which time we will have reached full aircrew manning.'

In late 2009 AH Force Headquarters at Wattisham and Joint Helicopter Command (JHC) at Erskine Barracks in Wilton conducted a review of AH training and the most efficient way to produce trained squadrons for operations. As a result it was decided to permanently attach AMTAT to 656 Squadron and remove it from the force cycle or rotation of squadrons to Afghanistan. It has since concentrated on running CTR and PDT training for the remaining five AH squadrons, in a similar way to RAF operational conversion units.

After the full force of six Apache squadrons had been trained, it was intended that ATIL would then move to pumping out a steady stream of new personnel to replace natural wastage of people from the Apache force.

'We are now moving to a steady state model,' said Godfrey. 'The course is mature and it has delivered exactly what the AH regiments wanted.'

Chapter 17

The Future of British Army Airpower

After a tumultuous decade at the centre of the campaigns in the Balkans, Iraq and Afghanistan, the helicopters and unmanned aerial vehicles of the Army Air Corps and Royal Artillery are now firmly established in the British Army. In the October 2010 UK Strategic Defence and Security Review (SDSR) the British Army's airpower remained largely unaffected by the swingeing cuts announced by the country's coalition government. This is testimony to their continuing commitment to the Afghan campaign.

The next decade is expected to see several major developments to enhance the fighting capabilities of British Army air units. At the heart of these is the imminent introduction of the Thales Watchkeeper unmanned aerial vehicle and in 2014 the arrival of the AgustaWestland Lynx Wildcat helicopter.

The Watchkeeper system is scheduled to begin replacing the Hermes 450 in 32nd and 47th Regiments Royal Artillery during 2012. Once the first batteries are fully trained they will gradually begin to replace the Hermes 450 in Afghanistan.

The Watchkeeper system has more advanced features than the Hermes 450, with the WK450 air vehicle boasting automatic take-off and landing, some seventeen hours' endurance, as well as a greater range of sensors. These include the CoMPASS electro-optic observation system, supplied by El-op (a subsidiary of Elbit), which incorporates thermal night vision and television cameras, as well as an eye-safe laser rangefinder, diode-pumped laser designator, laser target illuminator and autotracker. It will also have an I-Master SAR/GMTI radar, supplied by Thales Aerospace to provide wide area surveillance. The performance of these sensors is far in advance of any UAV-mounted sensors in the British armed forces and will result in a dramatic improvement in the Royal Artillery's battlefield surveillance capability.

The Lynx Wildcat will have a central role in British Army intelligence, surveillance, reconnaissance and targeting operations on future battlefields. (AgustaWestland)

Unlike the leased Hermes 450, the fifty-four Watchkeepers are being procured with all the necessary support equipment to allow the British Army to operate them without contractor support in front-line areas. This will mean that Royal Artillery will be able to operate Watchkeeper in theatres other than Afghanistan. Crucially, Watchkeeper will be available for the first time in the UK and elsewhere to support routine training exercises by the British Army. Blocks of airspace have been established over training areas on Salisbury Plain in Wiltshire and at Sennybridge in Wales. Aberporth airport in Wales and Boscombe Down airfield in Wiltshire are being prepared for Watchkeeper operations and Upavon airfield is to be used to practise grass

Test flights of the Lynx Wildcat are well underway at AgustaWestland's Yeovil plant in Somerset. (AgustaWestland)

field operations. The ability of Watchkeeper units to train with the British Army and RAF units on UK training areas will be a major development that will increase the combat effectiveness of units preparing for tours of duty in Afghanistan. They previously had to use very basic recorded imagery or lease light aircraft from commercial operators equipped with cameras and downlinks.

The AAC is on the verge of major changes as the Lynx AH.7/9s are replaced by the Future Lynx, or Lynx Wildcat as it has been re-branded, from 2014.

Although at times it has seemed as if the Lynx Wildcat would be cancelled, the project is now in its final phases with production well underway at the AgustaWestland plant in Yeovil in Somerset.

The helicopter will feature a nose-mounted thermal imaging camera and two very powerful LHTEC CTS800-4N turboshaft engines, which provide much improved performance over the old Lynx AH.7.

Upgrades to the Apache AH.1 play an important part in future AAC plans.
(Tim Ripley)

AgustaWestland AW159 Lynx Wildcat

Crew:	2 or 3
Capacity:	7 passengers
Length:	15.24m (50ft)
Rotor diameter:	12.80m (42ft)
Height:	3.73m (12.2ft)
Disc area:	128.7m^2 (1,385ft^2)
Maximum take-off weight:	6,000kg (13,200lb)
Powerplant:	2 × LHTEC CTS800-4N turboshaft, 1,015kW (1,362shp) each
Maximum speed:	291km/h (157 knots, 184mph)
Range:	777km (420NM) / 963 km (520NM) with auxiliary fuel
Endurance:	4 hr 30 min with auxiliary fuel
Armament:	forward firing CRV7 rockets and machine guns, Pintle mounted machine gun (e.g. FN MAG or Browning M2), air-to-surface missile system (possibly Hellfire in quad launchers [13])

Under the current outline, it is envisaged that 1 and 9 Regiment will eventually operate the Lynx Wildcat from a single 'super' base to be established at Yeovilton in Somerset. This will be co-located with the Royal Navy's Future Lynx force to allow a large and efficient depth maintenance support facility to be set up. It is hoped that this facility will ensure that the smaller number of Lynx Wildcats will be more 'available' than the current larger fleet of older Lynx. It is envisaged that each AAC Wildcat regiment will have two or three squadrons who will operate aircraft drawn from a central pool. The Royal Marines-tasked 847 Naval Air Squadron will also draw aircraft from this pool.

Originally, the Ministry of Defence ordered seventy Lynx Wildcats – forty for the AAC and thirty for the Royal Navy, with an option for another ten helicopters, but in 2008 it emerged that numbers had been reduced to thirty-four aircraft to the army and twenty-eight to the navy, reductions of six and two aircraft, respectively. In 2011 the Ministry of Defence increased the size of the AAC Lynx Wildcat order by four aircraft.

The arrival of the Lynx Wildcat will allow the retirement of the Lynx AH.7 and the Gazelle but the twenty-two Lynx AH.9As are expected to soldier on

The Thales Watchkeeper is scheduled to enter service during 2012 with the Royal Artillery. (Thales)

until at least the end of the decade. These are relatively young helicopters, which were only delivered in 1988, and received an added lease of life when they were upgraded in 2009–10.

Not surprisingly, the SDSR confirmed that the AgustaWestland Apache AH.1 would remain as the centre of the AAC's strike power.

Future upgrades to the UK's fleet of sixty-seven Apache AH.1s are unlikely to gather momentum until the last half of the next decade, after an assessment phase of the upgrade is scheduled to commence in the financial year 2012–13.

Senior UK Ministry of Defence and industry Apache programme managers have said that the funding issues and the need to keep helicopters in front-line service in Afghanistan in the near future means the UK will not immediately follow the US Army to convert its sixty-seven Apache to

Enhanced sensors and flight performance of the Watchkeeper will transform the Royal Artillery's unmanned aerial vehicle force. (Thales)

the Block III standard, particularly the incorporation of an open architecture computer system to allow 'plug and play' integration of new weapons and systems.

Air Commodore Doug Whittaker, DE&S Apache Programme Team Leader said that 'There is no doubt that we will have to do a detailed review of how we sustain the Apache to its out of service date of 2030 and beyond.'

He said that the current computer hardware and software that drives the UK Apache was 'adequate' for the immediate future but the helicopter would become increasingly expensive to support over the next decade. Whittaker predicted that such an upgrade would be needed in 'mid decade' when the US Army stops supporting its Block 1 airframes. A major factor in any future upgrade path for the Apache is the selection by the UK of a next generation guided weapon to replace the current Lockheed Martin AGM-114 Hellfire missile.

As well as enhancing the capabilities of its helicopters and UAVs, the British Army is moving to improve the efficiency of it air operations in complex battlefield environments. Real-time command and control of fixed wing aircraft, helicopters and UAVs in crowded airspace above battlefields

New ground stations will control the Watchkeepers as they operate over future battlefields. (Thales)

is vital to ensure none of them fly into each other by accident or fall victim to so-called 'friendly fire' from the ground or the air. Up to now the British Army has relied on RAF or USAF Boeing E-3 Sentry AWACS radar aircraft to generate what is known as a recognized air picture or RAP across a network of Link 16 data links. This is a real-time picture of all aircraft over a battlefield that is constantly updated from multiple sources.

To reduce reliance on AWACS, which may or may not be available due to other taskings, the Royal Artillery's Ground Based Air Defence (GBAD) organization decided to move ahead with the Land Environment Air Picture Provision (LEAPP) project in 2008. This is envisaged as an evolution of the British Army's RAP units that were stood up early this decade to provide land forces with access to Link 16 networks, generated by other agencies or systems.

LEAPP takes the concept further and also incorporates Saab Microwave Giraffe radars to generate sensor data to flow into the RAP and makes it relatively a stand-alone capability. Lockheed Martin UK are under contract to deliver the LEAPP capability by 2012.

Mick Halloran, Lockheed Martin UK/INSYS's Director of C4ISTAR said that LEAPP does more than just provide connectivity for UK air defence fire assets. He said it would provide the British Army with a 'cutting edge' capability. 'There is nothing else like it in Europe,' he said. 'This is less about defence and more about situational awareness of where blue forces are, understanding what is happening in the air space around you.'

MBDA's Fire Shadow loitering munitions will provide the Royal Artillery with a new type of aerial weapon. (MBDA)

Loitering munitions such as the Fire Shadow incorporate many of the advanced features of twenty-first century unmanned aerial vehicles. (MBDA)

The next decade is also likely to see the first British Army UAVs being fitted with weapons to speed their ability to bring firepower rapidly to bear against battlefield targets.

In the spring of 2010 British Army commanders began developing requirements that could see the service's UAVs armed with weapons to allow them to fly close air support missions in Afghanistan.

Dubbed Project Wasp, the effort is meant to fill capabilities gaps that have emerged because of the heavy tasking outside of the British Army area of responsibility in Helmand province of the Royal Air Force's armed General Atomics MQ-9 Reaper UAVs. This has left gaps in armed UAV coverage over UK ground troops on several occasions, say British Army officers who have served in Afghanistan in 2010.

Capability planners in the UK Ministry of Defence then began to consider the request from the British Army to formally endorse the requirements, which would see the installation of Thales Lightweight Multirole Missile (LMM) weapons. Senior army officers said they proposed three options, including urgent operational requirements to fit LMMs to Hermes 450s immediately and then the migration of the capability onto the Watchkeeper 450 in time for when it deploys to Afghanistan in 2012. There is also a potentially a longer term requirement to fill the emerging Scavenger-armed UAV requirement in the 2015–17 time frame that an enhanced Watchkeeper could fill.

Senior British Army generals have also expressed a desire to arm future generations of mini-UAVs so every British infantry company will be able to call down its own airborne firepower.

In the spring of 2010 the British Army made its first order for a new type of weapon, dubbed a loitering munition that takes the armed UAV concept one step further. The Royal Artillery hope it will give them the same firepower as the RAF's airliner-sized Reaper air vehicle for a fraction of the cost.

British engineers at missile company MBDA's Stevenage site in Herefordshire are working on the revolutionary design in co-operation with French experts, after the then Defence Secretary, Bob Ainsworth, gave the go ahead for production of the first batch last month to ensure troops in Afghanistan have the weapon by 2012. The drone made its first test flight at Aberporth in Wales in 2008. This is the first time the British military have ordered disposable air-launched weapons and Israel is the only other country that has this type of weapon in front-line service.

Fire Shadow is to be light enough to be fired from a small trailer and once in the air will patrol or 'loiter' over battle zones for up to ten hours at a time watching for the enemy activity. Television cameras will alert an operator back at the control station, who will then give the order to launch the Fire Shadow's on-board weapons. It carries a pack of miniature-guided missiles inside an internal weapon bay. If a target is not found, the Fire Shadow will be directed fly to an uninhabited area where it will be crashed and its warhead will be detonated so it won't become a danger to civilians.

The British Army is the largest operator of unmanned aerial in the UK armed forces and this is expected to continue for the foreseeable future. (Thales)

The delivery of the first Watchkeeper to the British Army in 2011 will dramatically increase the capability of its airpower. (Thales)

The British Army wants the Fire Shadow to be light and compact enough to be carried inside a Chinook battlefield transport helicopters so it can be used from remote areas where it is impossible to build a runway needed to launch bigger UAVs like the RAF's Reapers.

The first version of the Fire Shadow is expected to have a range of 100 kilometres and MBDA says it is looking to development future versions with longer ranges and more advanced on-board weapon packs beyond the basic fragmentation warhead. These could include warheads designed to kill enemy troops in the open, static or moving vehicles and hardened bunkers to give the Fire Shadow's operators the ability to attack different types of targets on a single mission.

It is hoped that the Fire Shadow will cost well below £100,000 each once production is running at full pace, compared with the £4 million American-made Reaper.

A Ministry of Defence expert involved in the project said:

> As well as being cheap and deadly, the Fire Shadow is designed to put the frighteners on enemy troops by buzzing around over their positions for hours at time until they are too scared to do anything for fear of getting a missile heading their way if they break cover.

The future of British Army airpower looks secure, with new helicopters, UAVs and other equipment coming into service over the next decade. The days of 'Teeny Weeny Airways' are a thing of the past. Perhaps even more important than its new equipment, the British Army has clearly become 'air minded' and thinks about using air assets as an integral part of almost everything it does. Central to making the British Army's soldiers believe they can rely on air support, from helicopters or UAVs, is the fact that it is flown by or operated by fellow soldiers who understand what it is like to be pinned down in a ditch under enemy fire.

This idea that British Army airpower is part of the Army and under Army control 24/7 is an anathema to some senior air force officers who believe in the centralized control and direction of airpower. Their success on the battlefields of the Balkans, Iraq and Afghanistan, has vindicated the British Army's approach to using air support. It also means that the AAC and Royal Artillery will remain in the forefront of providing air support for the British Army for many years to come.

Postscript – Apache Strike

At 1.04 a.m. on Saturday 4th June, the pilot of an Apache helicopter-gunship hidden in the inky black sky, pressed the trigger of the 30mm cannon, bringing down concentrated fire on a pick-up truck and ripping it open. Ammunition stored inside set off secondary explosions, spreading the swirling flames. Three men who had been trying to open fire with the vehicle's anti-aircraft gun, mounted at the back of the truck, were now terrified, scrambling to get away.

Pooled Media News Report from HMS Ocean

The first ever offensive operation by UK Army Air Corps AgustaWestland Apache AH.1 attack helicopters embarked on a warship in the early hours of 4 June 2011 and was the culmination of a joint Royal Navy and British Army effort to bring rotary wing combat power within range of Libya. This attack came three months after UK and NATO forces had been committed to action in the North African country following an insurrection against the forty-year rule of Colonel Muammar Gaddafi.

Under the code name Operation Cougar, the Royal Navy's Response Force Task Group (RFTG), commanded by Commodore John Kingwell, set sail for the Mediterranean Sea from a number of UK ports during April. It eventually boasted some fifteen helicopters, more than 2,000 personnel embarked on eight Royal Navy warships and Royal Fleet Auxiliary (RFA) support ships,

In a prepared statement released in early April, the UK Ministry of Defence said:

> ... the RFTG will be poised to respond to short notice tasking across a diverse range of defence activities such as non-combatant evacuation operations, disaster relief, humanitarian aid or amphibious operations. This deployment is not linked to events in Libya, which involve other elements of the UK Armed Forces.

The deployment of the RFTG to the Mediterranean and Middle East had been planned as a routine exercise but just as it was sailing a Royal Navy spokesman confirmed that 'world events' had prompted the British government to bring the sailing of the warships forward by three weeks.

The first elements of the RFTG, led by the amphibious ship HMS *Albion*, the Type 23 frigate HMS *Sutherland* and the landing ship RFA *Cardigan Bay*, sailed on 6 April and they spent most of May carrying out amphibious training on the UK Sovereign Base Areas on Cyprus. They included troops from 40 Commando making beach landings using landing craft and BAE Systems Viking armoured all-terrain vehicles, supported by Westland Sea King HC.4 support helicopters from 845 Naval Air Squadron and Westland Lynx Mk.7 liaison and observation helicopters of B Flight of 847 Naval Air Squadron.

The second wave of the RFTG sailed at the end of April led by the helicopter carrier HMS *Ocean*, with four Apache attack helicopters of 656 Squadron AAC, more HC.4 support helicopters of 845 Naval Air Squadron and a pair of Westland Sea King ASaC.7 airborne command and control helicopters of 857 Naval Air Squadron embarked. Sailing with HMS *Ocean* was the landing ship RFA *Mounts Bay*, the fast fleet tanker RFA *Wave*

Army Air Corps Apache during training for operations from Royal Navy warships, skills that were put into action from June 2011. (AgustaWestland)

The AgustaWestland Apache AH.1 proved a potent and effective strike weapon during maritime operations from HMS *Ocean*. (AgustaWestland)

Knight and replenishment ship RFA *Fort Rosalie*. As HMS *Ocean* entered the Mediterranean, her Apache carried out the first live firing of Hellfire missiles from attack helicopters embarked on a Royal Navy warship, as well as test firing their 30mm cannons and CRV-7 rockets. In mid-May this group of ships linked up with the advanced amphibious force, to complete the RFTG and conduct work-up training off Albania.

The helicopters on HMS *Ocean* and *Albion* had by then been combined into a Tailored Air Group (TAG) led by a command team provided by the UK's Joint Helicopter Command (JHC). The team had been working up options for using the TAG in the Libyan campaign, in conjunction with NATO fixed wing strike aircraft and French helicopters assets embarked on the assault ship FNS *Tonnerre*, which had set sail from Toulon for central Mediterranean on 20 May.

On 27 May, UK Prime Minister David Cameron agreed to proposals from Britain's Chief of Defence Staff, General Sir David Richards, to commit the TAG to NATO's Operation Unified Protector. Preparation now began in earnest for the British and French helicopters to join the action in Libya. Planning teams were dispatched from the helicopter units to the NATO Combined Air Operations Centre (CAOC) at Poggio Renatico in central Italy to co-ordinate their efforts with alliance fixed wing air units that would support them over Libya. Communications plans were put in place with the CAOC staff and the latest intelligence on targets was collected to be taken back to the pilots who would fly over Libya.

An intelligence, surveillance, target acquisition and reconnaissance (ISTAR) plan was developed to put the first tranche intended targets of the British and French attack helicopters under around the clock surveillance from NATO reconnaissance aircraft – led by RAF Raytheon Sentinel R.1 airborne stand-off radar aircraft – to build a picture of Libyan forces deployed around them. This was to try to reduce the number of surprises the attack helicopters might encounter on their first mission.

The complex effort to build the strike plan and ensure all the players – both rotary and fixed wing – were fully coordinated took several days and it was not until the first days of June that HMS *Ocean* and FNS *Tonnerre* and their escorts were off the coast of the Libyan town of Brega ready to strike.

The first UK attack helicopter operation involved a precision strikes against a Gaddafi regime radar installation and a military checkpoint, both located around Brega, with AGM-114 Hellfire missiles and 30mm cannon. The UK Ministry of Defence reported that both targets were destroyed and the helicopters then returned safely to HMS *Ocean*.

French Army Light Aviation (ALAT) Eurocopter EC625 Tiger HAP and Aerospatiale SA342 Gazelle attack helicopters went into action at almost the same time and destroyed a command and control post and fifteen military vehicles at on the eastern edge of Brega.

Supporting the helicopter strikes, was a fixed wing package of RAF ground attack aircraft, which destroyed another military installation in eastern Libya, whilst a separate RAF mission also attacked two ammunition bunkers at the large Waddan depot in central Libya.

Throughout these operations, a Sea King ASaC.7 of 857 Squadron was airborne providing command and control co-ordination for both the helicopters and fixed wing jets, as well as monitoring Libya vehicle movements with its Searchwater radar in ground moving target indicator mode. Overall command and control for the British and French helicopter strikes was provided by RAF, French, NATO and USAF Boeing E-3 Sentry airborne warning and command systems (AWACS) aircraft.

The British Apache helicopters reportedly received fire from Libya troops armed with AK-47s but none hit them. After a period of maintenance back on HMS *Ocean*, there was a further strike in the early hours of 5 June in the Brega area by two Apache, with a Sea King ASaC.7 helicopter providing

British and French attack helicopters closely co-ordinated their strike operations against Libya targets with NATO fixed wing attack aircraft, such as this RAF Panavia Tornado GR4. (Tim Ripley)

intelligence, which destroyed a multi-barrelled rocket launcher mounted on a truck and placed in an abandoned building.

For the leaders of the rebel resistance to Colonel Gaddafi, the first wave of British and French attack helicopter strikes took place in what they considered to be the wrong place. The focus of rebel efforts was to punch through the lines of Libyan government troops defending the strategic town of Zlitan, to the west of the rebel strong hold of Misrata. According to the rebels, if Zlitan could be taken then the road to Gaddafi's capital, Tripoli, would be open. They made repeated requests for NATO attack helicopters to join the alliance's aerial assault on their enemy's positions outside Zlitan.

On 9 June, the rebels requests were met when HMS *Ocean* moved up to the coast to Misrata and launched Apache helicopters to attack a regime military communications installation and multiple rocket launcher near the city. According to the UK Ministry of Defence the targets had been identified by NATO surveillance operations. Both targets were destroyed and the helicopters returned safely to HMS *Ocean*, said the ministry refuting Libyan government claims that had shot down a NATO helicopter in the region.

As with the previous Apache strikes around Brega, this further attack was integrated with a package of RAF Panavia Tornado GR4 and Eurofighter Typhoon aircraft, which destroyed four main battle tanks around Zlitan. To the south of Misrata the RAF also attacked a Libyan army transporter near Bani Walid.

UK and French attack helicopters then embarked on a concerted raiding strategy along the length of the Libya coast line to keep regime forces off balance and uncertain where the next attack will come from, according to AAC commanders involved in the mission to the North African country.

'AH attacks are visible demonstration of NATO resolve,' Lieutenant Colonel Phillip Cook, head of the Joint Helicopter Command (JHC) Air Manoeuvre Planning Team (AMPT) told a media briefing in the Ministry of Defence on 8 July.

> We are operate from Brega [on the eastern edge of regime controlled territory] to Zuwaya [between the capital Tripoli and the Tunisian border]. This increases the risk and sense of uncertainty among regime forces. This provides a vital psychological effect.

An AAC officer who served on HMS *Ocean* off Libya said:

> In a 24 hour period *Ocean* and *Tonnerre* can appear anywhere on the Libyan coast and then the regime will not know where we will strike next. Over the first 30 days of the operations we or French helicopters have been in action for 20 to 25 nights somewhere in Libya.

Cook, who led a team of AAC planners working at the CAOC at Poggio Renatico airbase to integrate helicopter and fixed wing air assets, said that between 3 June and 3 July the UK Apache had flown thirty sorties as part of thirteen strike missions and had carried out over thirty engagements against Gaddafi regime technical vehicles, check points, main battle tanks, coastal radars and special forces patrol boats.

'Not insignificant' mission co-ordination of UK and French AH mission takes place in the CAOC, combining UK and NATO fast jet strike aircraft, unmanned aerial vehicles (UAV), airborne command and control, suppression of enemy air defence and joint personnel recovery assets, into a single package, said Cook.

He described a typical attack helicopter mission off the besieged Libya city of Misrata in June. 'Our Apache were on deck alert on HMS *Ocean* off

Controllers on RAF and NATO AWACS radar aircraft provided command and control for AAC Apache strikes during the Libyan conflict. (Tim Ripley)

Misrata before a planned mission.' Royal Navy Westland Sea King ASaC.7s detected regime special forces patrol boats and then cued the attack helicopters to attack them. Cook said:

> The Apache then continued on their pre-planned mission against two vehicle check points. While this was happening a UAV located ZSU-23-4 self-propelled anti-aircraft system. Then they hit another check point and destroyed a technical vehicle.

During operations over Libya, AAC officers say their Apache have come under fire from anti-aircraft artillery and manportable shoulder launched surface-to-air missiles. One officer rebutted criticism from rebel fighters that the Apache were not being committed en masse to the battles around Misrata because of the threat from pro-regime ZSU-23-4s. The AAC officer said:

> We never underestimate the enemy's capability. We take all necessary precautions in planning so we do not get aircraft into difficulty. It is a risk versus reward issue. We will not win in Libya by winning a few tactical victories [around Misrata]. We are looking to win the wider campaign.

Cook said that the core of the helicopter force on HMS *Ocean* was provided by 87 AAC and Royal Electrical and Mechanical Engineers (REME) personnel assigned to 656 Squadron AAC. This unit is the AAC's dedicated conversion to role sub-unit and is also held at readiness to undertake 'bespoke small scale focus intervention' missions. He said the squadron had twelve aircrew and five Apache onboard HMS *Ocean* at the end of June.

Cook said that close co-operation with Royal Navy and Royal Air Force ISTAR is an integral part of AH operations off Libya. He said:

> ISTAR is a multi-layer package. RAF Sentinel R.1 airborne stand-off radar aircraft fly missions before our Apache launch and the crews on HMS *Ocean* look at the imagery after it is emailed to ship via the CAOC.

During and after Apache missions, a pair of 857 Naval Air Squadron Sea King ASaC.7s monitor the local area with their Thales Searchwater radars looking from emerging land and maritime threats. In the first months of operations the Sea King detachment on HMS *Ocean* has flown some 200 hours.

Apache operations against Libya from HMS *Ocean* opened a new chapter in the history of the Army Air Corps. (AgustaWestland)

Also embarked on HMS *Ocean* were four Westland Lynx AH.7s of 847 Naval Air Squadron, which were used for utility duties between Royal Navy and NATO ships off Libya. Westland Sea King HC.4s of 845 Naval Air Squadrons that originally deployed when she sailed from the UK in April were withdrawn from duty on HMS *Ocean* at the end of June.

The UK Apache AH.1 force attacked more than 100 targets during their participation in the Libya campaign up to mid August 2011, according to Lt Col Jason Etherington, commanding officer of 4 Regiment AAC. The five Apache attack helicopters on HMS *Ocean* fired 99 Hellfire missiles and 16 Bristol Aerospace CRV-7 rockets, destroying 107 targets, including 54 'technical' armed vehicles and two rigid inflatable boats.

In addition, the helicopters, which flew some 75 combat hours in 49 individual aircraft sorties during operations against Libya and fired some 4,100 rounds of 30mm cannon ammunition. Etherington said that the Apache had planned to fly some 44 'strike missions' during the Libya operation but half of them had been cancelled for a variety of reasons.

Etherington said 'We struck every target we were tasked for by the CAOC. Our five Apache did not win war on their own. We were just another tool. The key was our psychological effect. There is evidence in open source that people (in Libya) were turning around saying they were terrified of an Apache appearing behind their frontlines. We proved we could go on a ship and operate, we validated it.'

269

Glossary

AAC: Army Air Corps (British Army)
AB: Airbase
ANA: Afghan National Army
ANAAC: Afghan National Army Air Corps
ASTOR: Airborne Stand Off Radar (UK)
Avn: Aviation (US Army)
AWACS: Airborne Warning and Control System
Bn: Battalion
CAB: Combat Aviation Brigade (US Army)
CAOC: Combined Air Operations Centre (USAF)
CIA: Central Intelligence Agency (USA)
CMND: Canadian Ministry of National Defence
CSAR: Combat Search and Rescue
Det: Detachment
ELINT: Electronic intelligence
EOG: Expeditionary Operations Group (USAF)
FAC: Forward Air Controller
FARP: Forward Arming and Refuelling Point
Flt: Flight
FOB: Forward Operating Base
IADS: Integrated Air Defence System
ISTAR: Intelligence, surveillance, target acquisition and reconnaissance
JHF(1):   Joint Helicopter Force (Iraq) (UK)
JHF(A):   Joint Helicopter Force (Afghanistan) (UK)
JSFAW: Joint Special Forces Aviation Wing (UK)
JTF-Afg: Joint Task Force-Afghanistan (Canada)
JTAC: Joint Terminal Attack Controller (US)
KFOR: Kosovo Force (NATO)
Manpad: Manportable surface-to-air missile
MND(SE):   Multi-National Division (South East) (UK)
NAEWF: NATO Airborne Early Warning Force
NATO: North Atlantic Treaty Organization
NAS: Naval Air Squadron (UK)
RA: Royal Artillery
RAF: Royal Air Force (UK)
Regt: Regiment
SAM: Surface-to-air missile
SAS: Special Air Service (UK and Australia)
SOAR: Special Operation Aviation Regiment (US Army)
SOF: Special Operations Forces (US Army)
SOG: Special Operations Group (USAF)
SOS: Special Operations Squadron (USAF)
SOW: Special Operations Wing (USAF)
Sqn: Squadron
TACP: Tactical Air Control Party
TF: Task Force
UAV: Unmanned aerial vehicle
USAF: US Air Force
USMC: US Marine Corps
USN: US Navy
UN: United Nations

Index